THINKING THROUGH CLASS DISCUSSION

Thinking through Class Discussion

a TECHNOMIC® publication

Published in the Western Hemisphere by
Technomic Publishing Company, Inc.
851 New Holland Avenue, Box 3535
Lancaster, Pennsylvania 17604 U.S.A.

Distributed in the Rest of the World by
Technomic Publishing AG
Missionsstrasse 44
CH-4055 Basel, Switzerland

Printed in the United States of America
10 9 8 7 6 5 4 3 2 1

Main entry under title:
Thinking through Class Discussion: The Hilda Taba Approach

A Technomic Publishing Company book
Bibliography: p. 109
Includes index p. 111

Library of Congress Catalog Card No. 93-60802
ISBN No. 1-56676-055-0

THINKING THROUGH CLASS DISCUSSION

THE HILDA TABA APPROACH

Mary C. Durkin

TECHNOMIC
PUBLISHING CO., INC.

LANCASTER · BASEL

To the classroom teacher

CONTENTS

IT was a fortunate coincidence that Dr. Hilda Taba joined the staff of San Francisco State at the same time the Director of Curriculum of Contra Costa County Department of Education in California was searching for a consultant whose mode of thinking was compatible with the staff's wishes to write a social studies teachers' guide.

The Contra Costa County Board of Education provided Dr. Taba with ample time by not setting a deadline for the guides. Seven years of work were spent on two studies of children's thinking and the teachers' guides. The process included conferences with content specialists, in-service workshops, and the writing, tryout, and rewriting of the guides. Once produced, the guides were well received, not only in Contra Costa County, but wherever they became known. A third study evaluated and extended the program. All three studies were funded by the U.S. Department of Education, Health, and Welfare, Office of Education, Bureau of Research.

From the work of classroom teachers and my co-workers in curriculum came the contributions that have made this book possible. They are so numerous that it is impossible to give recognition to each by name. But a special debt is due the late Evelyn Jegi Blodgett, Director of Curriculum, who recognized in Dr. Taba's thinking the consultant her staff would welcome. Many thanks to my co-worker Alice Duvall who always shared her ideas generously with me. I am especially indebted to Dr. Norman Wallen of San Francisco State University for his careful reading of the manuscript, his carefully thought-out suggestions, and his enthusiasm for the book. Thanks are due also to Dr. Jack Fraenkel of San Francisco State University for his encouragement and suggestions. Special mention must be made of the contribution to the book by the following classroom teachers: Kim Ellis, Patsy Tanabe Endsley, Pat Hardy, Sue Harper, Irene Schulte, Mary Shindelus, and Bob Nabuo Watanabe.

Appreciation is due the publishers who gave permission to quote from their publications. And last, but not least, is the careful work of Anne Mauro who put the manuscript through her word processor, sketched diagrams when she did not understand mine, and alerted me to passages that the lay person might not understand.

OBJECTIVES OF THE BOOK

THE material in this book is based on the thinking of Dr. Hilda Taba and her staff members as they formulated strategies for leading students to improve the quality of their thinking. It includes examples of skills demonstrated by trained teachers leading a class discussion using identified strategies, as well as examples of the problems a teacher may have in his/her implementation of discussion procedures. The section in each chapter labeled "Points for Thought" and the chapter titled "As Others See It" were formulated from materials developed for teachers being introduced to procedures in inductive teaching.

The objectives of the book are:

- to provide typescripts of classroom discussions for study by all those who work directly or indirectly with children in situations where helping children learn to think is a goal of their work—teachers, docents in museums, storytellers in libraries, authors of textbooks, writers of captions, curriculum writers, producers of teaching films, filmmakers for children's programs, and instructors in college classes that include analysis of children's thinking as part of their content
- to present strategies for classroom teachers that assist them in their goal of teaching children to think—a goal not achieved in any one year but one that should be supported every year in a student's school life
- to impress all who add to a child's store of learning with the importance of inviting him/her to venture beyond memorization of facts to seeking out properties, discovering relationships, and developing inferences
- to emphasize that acceptance of each child's contribution in a discussion by teacher and peer adds to his/her self-esteem

- to assure teachers and others who lead discussions that group discussions can become a learning situation for all and an opportunity for each child to express his/her inferences and feelings
- to encourage curriculum writers to explore further the Taba model as a process guide in the social studies

DR. HILDA TABA AND HER THEORIES OF LEARNING AND CURRICULUM

Dr. Hilda Taba, Professor of Education at San Francisco State University and internationally recognized authority in the field of human relations and curriculum development, was born in Estonia. She received her degree from the University of Tartu in 1926 and came to the United States in 1926 as a European Fellow of Bryn Mawr College, where she received her master's degree. Continuing her studies in the United States, she earned a Ph.D. degree from Teachers College, Columbia University.

Returning to Estonia in 1930, Dr. Taba taught in the Education Department at the Home Economics College. In 1933 Dr. Taba returned to the United States to be an instructor in German at the Dalton School and remained there until 1935. She served on the faculties of Ohio State University and the University of Chicago before coming to San Francisco State in 1951.

During her consultancy on the social studies curriculum in Contra Costa County in California, she found tremendous support within the County Board of Education and the County Schools Office, and among the teachers and administrators. Her work soon involved schools in other counties of the San Francisco Bay area.

Dr. Taba developed the theory that the most durable form of knowledge lies in concepts and ideas, and therefore, the focus of the social studies curriculum should center on those ideas and concepts that are accepted widely by specialists in the various disciplines. In response to those who tended to base their rationale on some single criterion of content or child development as they designed curricula, Dr. Taba pointed out, "Obviously a curriculum has to do with teaching something to someone; hence, it can be neither entirely content-centered nor entirely child-centered." Over a period of seven years, classroom teachers, curriculum consultants, and content specialists working with Dr.

Taba developed, tested, and revised a series of teacher guides for a curriculum with the following characteristics:

(*1*) *Content is sampled rather than simply covered.* For instance, three colonies, each settled by people for different reasons, from different backgrounds, and with different resources are studied in depth rather than "covering" thirteen colonies superficially. The content sampled must be appropriate and sufficient to develop a ˙ major concept or main idea.

(*2*) *Study questions are intended to make certain that student research will include seeking out facts related to the main idea being studied.* Study questions should never limit a student's interest. Students are also encouraged to share facts that diverge from the idea presented.

(*3*) *Learning activities should:*
- be described in detail; teachers are given suggestions as to <u>what</u> they might do and how they could ensure the involvement of students. Available resources for information are given.
- be ordered sequentially; arranged from concrete to abstract; from familiar to remote
- be in "bite-sized" increments; some groups of students can move through a series of learning activities quickly while others need more time and smaller "bites"
- serve a range of objectives; concepts, skills, attitudes, and values
- provide for rotation of intake of information, organization of data and analysis of conclusions
- lead toward independent thinking by students

(*4*) *Evaluation should be a continuous process.* Diagnosis of difficulties and of readiness for the next step is more useful than a test at the end of the unit of study. Final tests should be only a small part of the total program of evaluation.

DR. TABA'S WRITINGS ON CURRICULUM

Dr. Taba and her colleagues produced two sets of curriculum guides for social studies. The first (grades 1–6) was made available by the Contra Costa County Office of Education; the second (grades 1–8) by the U.S. Department of Health, Education, and Welfare and by the Addison-Wesley Publishing Co. Neither set is currently in print; however either may be reproduced or used as a model. Printouts of the second set (grades 1–8) may be secured from ERIC, Clearinghouse for Social Studies, Social Studies Development Center, 2805 East Tenth Street, Suite 120, Indiana University, Bloomington, Indiana 47405.

A general introduction to the curriculum is available in the following sources: Taba, Hilda. *Curriculum Development: Theory and Practice.* Chapter 20, Harcourt, Brace and World, 1962; and Taba, Hilda et al. *A Teacher's Handbook to Elementary Social Studies (Second Edition),* Addison-Wesley Publishing Co., Reading, Massachusetts, 1971.

THE THINKING PROCESS

The 1950s and 1960s saw renewed attention to the question of how human thinking develops. Some studies of that period provided descriptions of styles of thinking, but these were not easily translated into methods for modifying ways of thinking. Dr. Taba was much influenced by the work of Jean Piaget and the Geneva school. The studies of the development of thought and intelligence by Piaget suggest that the evolution of thought takes place in three stages: (1) the sensory-motor stage or the stage of preverbal intelligence; (2) the stage of concrete operations or thinking with objects and concrete events, which lasts from two to eleven years of age; and (3) the stage of conceptual or formal thought which is established between eleven years of age and the end of adolescence. One of the research questions, however, was whether training would alter these age limits. It seemed reasonable to Dr. Taba that one could assume that if both the curriculum and teaching strategies were addressed to the development of thought, formal thought might appear earlier. Moreover, she hypothesized that with adequate strategies the possibility of abstract thought might be opened to students now considered to have too little intelligence to be capable of higher levels of mental activity.

Two studies, funded by grants from the Cooperative Research Branch of the U.S. Office of Education, were conducted by Dr. Taba. They focused on the possibility that students could be trained in the processes of higher-level thinking, provided that trainable cognitive skills could be identified. The studies confirmed her hypotheses; after training, students did follow the teacher's line of questioning up to the abstract level at an earlier age than untrained students had, and students thought to be "slow" often moved into the abstract level. When the teacher did not ask questions to elicit higher levels of thought, the students rarely raised their thinking automatically.

Teaching Thinking and Its Basic Tasks

In order to make thinking teachable, Dr. Taba and her team identified three cognitive tasks: developing concepts, developing inferences and generalizations, and the application of generalizations. The strategies developed for teaching these aspects of thought are provided in this book. In their simplest forms, the processes of these tasks are:

(*1*) Developing Concepts
  * differentiating the characteristics of objects and events (listing in response to a focused question)
  * abstracting common characteristics in an array of dissimilar objects or events (grouping on the basis of common characteristics)
  * discovering categories (labeling which involves subsuming, that is, deciding which diverse objects may be put under the same label)

(*2*) Developing Generalizations
  * evolving generalizations and principles from an analysis of concrete data (first organized by listing, grouping, and labeling)
  * explaining specific events (relating points of information to each other, such as why ocean currents affect temperature)
  * forming inferences (reaching insights that go beyond that which is directly given, such as inferring from the data on products the Bedouin sells and those he buys at the markets, that the herder of the desert and the people of the oasis need each other)

(*3*) Applying Generalizations
  * applying known principles and facts to explain new phenomena or predict consequences from known conditions (analyzing the problem and the conditions in order to determine which facts and principles are relative and which are not)
  * making a rational prediction or explanation (developing causal links between the condition and the prediction or explanation)

Examples of students applying and extending generalizations at which they have arrived are found in the following case.

A second-grade class studying services to their community developed a chart of workers and the services those workers needed. Through the teacher's questions they responded with these generalizations:

Class: A doctor can't take care of the sick persons all by himself. He needs lots of workers. Most workers have to have a lot of services so they can do their work. Some services are in the neighborhood but lots come from other places.

The teacher then presented the class with this situation:

Teacher: The city of (nearby) needs to enlarge the airport. If it is enlarged what might happen? (She sketched the outline of the airport and tower on the board. As children responded she sketched an outline or symbol for the prediction.)

Class: The children responded with: workers come ⟶ more houses ⟶ more rooms on our school ⟶ more stores ⟶ more airplanes come ⟶ more noise, etc.

In the studies on children's thinking conducted by Dr. Taba and her team, the term "generalization" refers to an inference (or conclusion) expressed in a sentence and arrived at by examining a number of facts. It is the end-product of the process of differentiating and generalizing.

The strategies formulated for discussion in the cognitive area and for those in the affective areas help the student direct his/her thinking from specific data to an idea arrived at inductively. This is not to deny that much learning can be attained by the deductive method or by rote. Too often educators have taken extreme positions between learning deductively or through discovery. Actually, the problem is what to "give" and what to "develop" in students. The curriculum developed in the Taba project used both methods but emphasized the inductive in the hope that, *through years of constructing inferences and generalizations, students will become logical and creative thinkers.* Below are examples of the inductive and deductive method.

Two teachers wished their classes to identify some of the characteristics of Cortés and to make general statements about them. The first teacher approached the task by asking, "From all you have read about Cortés, what kind of a person do you think he was?" In other words, she asked the students to make inferences in the opening question. Her class identified several characteristics, and she followed up on certain ones by asking "What did he do that made you think he was tricky?" and so on. This teacher was using a deductive questioning sequence, asking students to start by making inferences or conclusions and then to support them by reference to information studied.

The second teacher's opening questioning sequence was, "As you think of Cortés, what were some of the things he did?" She listed a number of Cortés' acts that the students remembered on the chalk- board. Next, she said, "Let's look at, for instance, his burning ships. What kind of person do you think would do this?" And "Let's think of Cortés as he wept in *The Sad Night*. What kind of person do you think would do this?" She pursued a number of Cortés' actions and then asked, "Now what kind of a person would you say Cortés was?" One child might see him as a man of strong character; another might see him as a man who was dishonest.

The second teacher was using an inductive questioning sequence. It provided the students with the opportunity to examine Cortés' acts before judging him. This teacher planned also to have her students see as many sides of his character as they could.

AFFECTIVE STRATEGIES

Since social studies are concerned with exploring values, attitudes, and feelings toward important topics and issues, there is a need for appropriate ways of probing emotions. It was recognized that comparatively little is known about the outcomes of in-school procedures in the affective area. Nevertheless, a considerable body of theory and some research suggested that it should be possible to devise teaching strategies to facilitate attainment of objectives in this domain. The three strategies presented in this book (Chapter 8) are:

Exploring Feelings

In this strategy students are encouraged to:

- make inferences as to how other people feel and why
- recognize the variety of possible emotional reactions to a given circumstance
- relate what happens to other persons (or groups) to emotional experiences they themselves have had

- explore reasons for emotional reactions
- compare their own feelings with those of others and, if appropriate, generalize to feelings of all people

Interpersonal Problem Solving

In this strategy students are presented with a problem situation involving conflict among persons or groups (e.g., playground disputes, disagreements over traditions) and are asked to:

- propose and defend solutions
- relate the events to similar experiences they have had
- evaluate the way of handling the recalled problem and consider various alternatives they might have followed

Analyzing Values

In this strategy students are asked to recall information about specified behavior on the part of an individual or group. Then they are asked to:

- explain why they think such behavior occurs (The questions are specific to types of behavior which indicate values, e.g., "Why do you suppose these people live near relatives?")
- infer what values are implicit in the behavior (This process is repeated for other groups and individuals.)
- make comparisons among the various values which have been discussed
- hypothesize about their own behavior and values

The reader will notice the overlap between these strategies and the cognitive strategies. This is intentional since it is hoped that cognitive skills will be applied to affective concerns and that attitudes and feelings enter into cognitive performance.

CLASSROOM DISCUSSION

Asking appropriate questions is probably the most effective art a teacher can acquire to help students become productive thinkers. In classroom discussions both students and teacher assume a variety of roles. While initially the teacher may see her main role as that of questioner, of no less importance is the bringing of his/her humanness to the discussion. In a discussion every child can make a contribution and be recognized for it. Many teachers continue to say that the strategies and the teacher's additional questions that extend the participation of students, such as, "Can you give us an example?" or "Does someone have something to add to what Maria has said?" etc., have simply become a way of teaching for them.

The subtle value of the class discussion is expressed well by Dr. Taba: "Class discussion can be used to break the closed tracks of thinking that an individual builds for himself. Properly used, group discussion is a means for preventing these tracks from hardening. To use personal expression from the entire group in developing an idea or a pattern of feeling is to open wider possibilities than any individual can build for himself."[1]

THE PLAN OF THE BOOK

In planning this book the author decided to follow the principles that seemed appropriate for teachers being introduced to Dr. Taba's strategies for helping children lift their level of thinking.

Content

The content related to the thinking strategies is basic information. It should be adequate, but not overwhelming. The reader should be introduced to one strategy at a time, making it a more manageable "bite."

Raw Data

The data necessary for analysis are found in transcripts of actual classroom discussions. The discussions were taped in the situations that classroom teachers face every day: tree-trimming outside the windows, fire-drills, latecomers. They were taped with teachers who had had two years of experience with the social studies program and also with those who had just entered the program.

[1]Taba, Hilda. 1962. *Curriculum Development: Theory and Practice.* New York: Harcourt, Brace and World, p. 375.

Interpretation

Questions in the "Points for Thought" sections seek to have the reader consider not only the response of each particular child, but also how the response might be related to what others said, how it might go beyond the data given, how the child might feel in light of the responses he/she receives from teacher and peers, the level of thinking demonstrated, and how the child's thinking might diverge from what others said.

A detailed technique for coding students' responses is not included in the book's content for two reasons: (1) the time required to acquire skill in coding is extensive, and (2) the classroom teacher would rarely have the time required to code children's contributions. However, a number of yardsticks that can be used easily and informally is provided.

Rotation

The rhythm of intake of information (reading the raw material and background material) and making interpretations that seem valid form a rotation that occurs in each chapter. Where appropriate, the teacher is asked to create his/her own sequence of questioning.

Affective Areas

Dr. Taba was concerned not only that social studies direct attention to the people of each area studied (e.g., those being affected by decisions of government, etc.), but that it also give attention to the student's developing self-concept. The writer hopes that several examples in this book will alert teachers to the importance of *all* contributions in classroom discussions being acknowledged and respected not only by the teacher but also by the student's peers.

Independent Thinking and How Others See It

To provide an "answer book" giving the right answer would not be in accord with Dr. Taba's philosophy unless it is related to a particular fact, not the products of thought. However, teachers are usually interested in the experiences of other teachers and in their ideas. So, from notes evaluating meetings, from written comments, and from memory we have included a final chapter titled "As Others See It" which shows how a variety of teachers have interpreted the information provided.

HOW THE BOOK MIGHT BE USED

The manner in which this book is used depends on the objectives of the person using it. The college instructor teaching students how to analyze children's thinking may wish to use the discussion sequences for that purpose only. Or a docent in a museum showing a particular picture or discussing artifacts of a culture the children had been studying might wish to use a discussion strategy to lead the children from the level of naming artifacts and their use to inferring their importance in the culture, or to what an historian might learn about the culture from the picture. Classroom teachers may wish to use the sample dialogues as a basis for devising discussions that impart one specific thinking skill.

Anyone intending to use discussion techniques with children should be concerned with the totality of what is happening to the child. When undertaking new techniques such a person needs suggestions and support from fellow workers. Taping and listening became a habit with many teachers participating in the Taba research. Many offered to demonstrate for each other. From our experience with the Taba curriculum we learned that a most productive approach is having two (or more) teachers observe and analyze one another's discussion techniques. It is hoped that this book will provide one means for all such teachers to improve and better understand the use of discussion.

CHAPTER 1

Classroom Atmosphere

CLIMATE THAT SUPPORTS PRODUCTIVE THINKING

DR. Taba made these points when she spoke of the classroom climate that supported productive thinking:

(*1*) Adults accept the probabilistic nature of knowledge. Each time a child uses "Probably he felt . . ." or "Maybe it could be . . ." he/she is recognizing that there could be a different cause or result, explanation or interpretation.

(*2*) The teacher fosters security that does not invite dependency. Each time students are asked to wrestle with a problem to which there is not an easy right or wrong answer and are asked "What do you think about this?", they are helped to release themselves from dependency on the book or what they have heard someone say.

(*3*) The child can afford to be honest. A child may feel trapped by a question a teacher meant to be open if he or she has reason to fear rejection. He may then avoid revealing what he really thinks or remain silent.

(*4*) All contributions are recognized and respected. Each time a child's contribution is recognized by his teacher or peer saying, "Well, like Jose said, . . .", Jose is a bit surer of himself and more willing to express himself the next time.

DISCUSSION SEQUENCE

Willie and His Cup of Coffee

Class Description

The following sequence was taped in a first-grade class in a school located in the agricultural area of California. Some of the children in

1

this school were migratory. Family income in the area was generally on the low end of the scale. The teacher, Ms. Milton, had been invited to participate in the Taba Curriculum Project because she was held in esteem by her co-workers and could be depended on to be open in her evaluation of materials being developed. She had attended one training session in which Dr. Taba emphasized the importance of a "comfortable atmosphere" in which children could express their thinking and feelings.

Focus of Activity

Ms. Milton decided to have the children draw a picture in response to a completely open-ended question so they could speak to it without thinking about right and wrong answers. The question was "What happened this morning?" She tape-recorded the children's remarks about their pictures. A short sequence follows:

[1] Ms. Milton: Jimmy Lee, tell the children what is happening in your picture.

Jimmy Lee: Well, this is the table and I'm eating breakfast and I'm eating oats and this is my coffee.

Ms. Milton: Coffee? A little boy like you is drinking coffee?

Jimmy Lee: Yes ma'am.

[5] Ms. Milton: Mary, tell the group what is happening in your picture.

Mary: This is me and I'm eating breakfast. This is my cornflakes and this is my coffee.

Ms. Milton: You, too, Mary? Does your mother let you drink coffee?

Mary: Yes ma'am. (voice low and speech tentative on tape)

Billy: Ms. Milton, I had coffee, too.

[10] Ms. Milton: Oh, no, Billy.

Billy: (belligerently) I did, too.

Ms. Milton: OK, Billy. That's all right.

Several children now show pictures of dressing, riding on the school bus, playing with the dog, etc. All acceptable. Then Ms. Milton called on Willie.

Willie: This is me drinking coffee and, Ms. Milton, you know why I'm drinking coffee?

Ms. Milton: No, Willie. Why?

[15] Willie: Doctor's orders. One cup a day.

Ms. Milton brought the tape to me after school that day and said, "Listen to what I'm doing to those children."

POINTS FOR THOUGHT

Signals of Discomfort in Children*

1. What reaction did Ms. Milton have when the first child mentioned coffee?
2. Why do many of us react in this way when a child gives an answer contrary to what is expected?
3. In what different ways do you feel the children seem affected?
4. Is there a point at which you think Ms. Milton realizes some children feel trapped?
5. What might a teacher listening to a taped discussion become aware of that may have evaded her while she was conducting the discussion?
6. List a couple of ways other than the teacher's words by which a child senses approval or disapproval.

*See Chapter 9, page 93.

CHAPTER 2

Strategy for Developing Concepts

LEADING CHILDREN TO DISCOVER COMMON CHARACTERISTICS AMONG ITEMS IN A GROUP

WHY is discussion so important in the classroom? Because, stresses Dr. Taba, so many children find writing very difficult and the teacher will never know what a child is thinking unless the child is given an opportunity to talk while the teacher listens.

Questioning is probably the most important teaching tool a teacher possesses. There are numerous kinds of classroom discussions: those that are spontaneous, stimulated by the sudden appearance of a rainbow or a butterfly, or by conflict on the playground; there are those in which committees share information gathered by using study questions; those that focus on helping a child lift the level of his thinking, help him express his feelings, or become sensitive to the feelings of others. There are also times to brainstorm, but each technique should meet the purpose of the discussion. Dr. Taba's remarks below are related to the use of thinking and/or feeling questioning strategies:

> The necessary information should be readily available to all students. A question that has only one right answer is asking a child to remember, not to lift his thinking.
>
> The words of a question in the strategy may be changed, but not the sequence. It is through the sequence of questioning that the child learns the structure of arriving at rational thought.
>
> A rapid-fire discussion is seldom thoughtful.
>
> Hang in with a student when he/she is attempting to clarify his/her thinking.
>
> Teachers are often committed to giving everyone a turn, but children do not think in turns. Be willing to stay with an individual.
>
> As a rule, teachers leading a discussion cannot endure silence. Try waiting at least five seconds for a child to think.

5

Teachers might well ask, "If I use a structured sequence, where does my skill as a leader come in?" Dr. Taba would have assured all teachers that the real skill of the teacher lies in her ability to read feedback while on her feet. She may then do any number of things—reword the question, give the child the needed data, give him an example, help the child rethink his response, or support him by putting an error or irrelevant statement in an easier context. In other words, the teacher assumes many roles as she reacts to the child. She also controls the process but never the content of what a child says unless the child's basic information is incorrect; then he/she needs to be given correct information immediately.

Dr. Taba held firmly that to be of value to the teacher, research on thinking had to be carried on in the classroom, and it had to identify levels of thinking children can attain in a large group situation. Such research had then to be translated into classroom procedures. Dr. Taba's investigations established a pattern of children following the level of a teacher's questioning as shown in Figure 2.1.[2]

Children rarely rose to a higher level of thought than the teacher's question required, but they followed the teacher's question into the abstract level at an earlier age than experiments not using a questioning strategy had shown.

One of the strategies developed by Dr. Taba and her colleagues is called Developing Concepts. This task requires students to group a number of items on some kind of basis. The teaching strategy consists of asking students, in sequence, the questions found in Table 2.1.

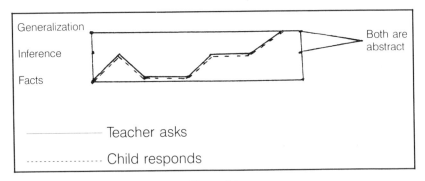

Figure 2.1.

[2]Taba, H., S. Levine and F. Elzey. 1964. *Thinking in Elementary School Children.* San Francisco, CA: San Francisco State College, U.S. Office of Educ., Coop. Res. Proj. No. 1574.

TABLE 2.1 Developing Concepts[a] — Listing, Grouping, and Labeling.

Teacher	Student	Teacher
What did you see (find, notice) here?	Gives items.	Makes sure items are accessible to all students. For example, pictures, chalkboard lists, transparency lists, individual lists, item cards.
Do any of these items (pictures) seem to belong together?[b]	Finds some similarity as a basis for grouping items.	Communicates grouping. For example, marks with symbols; underlines with colored chalk; arranges pictures or cards.
Why would you group them together?[c]	Identifies and verbalizes the common characteristics of items in a group.	Seeks clarification when necessary.
What would you call this group you have formed?	Verbalizes a label that appropriately encompasses all items.	Records.
Can we put some of these items in different groups? Why would you group them that way?[d]	States different relationships.	Communicates new grouping to class.

[a]See Norman E. Wallen, Mary C. Durkin, Jack R. Fraenkel, Anthony M. Naughton and Enoch I. Sawin. 1969. *Development of a Comprehensive Model for Social Studies of Grades One through Eight, Inclusive of Procedures for Implementation and Dissemination*, Final Report, Project No. 5-1314, Washington, D.C., U.S. Office of Education, Oct.

[b]As a "talk shorthand" Dr. Taba often referred to the "what" questions and the "why" questions. Many teachers understood this to mean that the questions should begin with those words. Not at all. The first question is meant to get out the basic facts to be used in discussion. Such responses come from memory—something the child observed happen, not what he thinks or feels about it.

Teachers had a variety of ways to handle the first question, such as having students work in small groups to list their responses to "From what you have heard and read about Cortés, I want you to list as many things as you can that he actually did." Then there was a sharing of lists which the teachers recorded on the chalkboard before they asked questions that required abstract responses.

[c]The word "why" seems threatening to some children. There are many ways to ask this question, such as, "I'm interested in how you decided to put those two things together. Tell me more."

[d]Although this step is important because it encourages flexibility, it will not be appropriate on all occasions. If the teacher is focusing on improving the children's attention to the questions, she may feel she will cause confusion by encouraging some children to suggest several different relationships they see for a word. Some children love to play games with words (and adults, too). (The *San Francisco Chronicle* carried an article in the Spring of 1990 on admissions to college and the work of committees. It reported that one student was found to be worthy of admission to Stanford because of his creative thinking. He had grouped "warts" and "friends" together because "they both grow on you.")

DISCUSSION SEQUENCE

My Family Spending Money

Class Description

The class consisted of twenty-six junior primary first graders. The kindergarten teachers had reported that these children paid little attention to directions or questions. There were nine girls and seventeen boys. Three were foreign-born and from bilingual homes. This video-taping was made in early May. At that time the spread was from a 1.1 grade score to a 2.4 grade score on a standard reading test.

Material

The pictures the children referred to had been drawn the day before the taping. They had been asked to draw a picture that showed the family or someone in the family spending money. For the discussion, the teacher placed the pictures along the ledge of the chalkboard. The children sat in a group close to the board.

Focus of Discussion

The discussion attempted: (1) to have the children focus on the question asked in identifying what the family spent money for; (2) to group pictures when they saw similarities among the way they spent money; and (3) to give the groups labels in their own words.

[1] **Teacher:** These are the pictures you drew yesterday about our families spending money. Look at your picture and think about it . . . (pause). Greg, would you like to talk about your picture?

Greg: We're buying and here's the road and there are some people crossing the street to come to buy shoes, too.

Teacher: Greg, for what purpose is your family spending money?

Greg: For shoes.

[5] **Teacher:** David Stuart, let's have you tell about your picture.

David S.: My dad bought stuff to take up in the mountains to work on a bridge at my grandma's house. Somebody ran into it and cracked it last week.

After sixteen children had responded, the teacher moved to the second part of the task.

Teacher: Let's take another look at these pictures. We're going to pin our pictures on the tackboard in little groups to show the different reasons these families are spending money.

Ricky: Mine should go with Michael's.

Teacher: Why do you want to put your tractor with Michael's new car?

[10] Ricky: Because my dad is buying something that is like a tractor piece.

Teacher: How is the tractor piece like the new car?

Ricky: It is something that helps the tractor go.

Teacher: Ohhh? The car helps the tractor go?

Ricky: No! The tractor piece helps the tractor go and the car has one too.

[15] Teacher: (sigh) Oh, I see. There is something in the tractor that is like something in the car. What is it?

Ricky: I don't know.

Teacher: I think you do. Who can help us out? Michael?

Michael: The engine.

Teacher: Yes, I think engine is the word you want, Ricky. Craig Allen, do you see some pictures that could go together?

[20] Craig: My picture of guns and the trailer picture could go together because they're both camping pictures.

Eddie: My trailer is for camping too. Put it with Randy's.

Teacher: All right. We'll put the guns and the two trailers together because they're all for camping. That should work out just fine. Diane, do you see some that should go together?

Diane: Mine and Betty's should go together.

Teacher: Why should yours and Betty's go together?

[25] Diane: Because they're both flowers.

Teacher: Let's think about this for a moment. Betty, why does your family spend money for plants?

Betty: To make the yard look nice.

Teacher: Skip, do you see others that go together?

Skip: Mine and Kim's.

[30] Teacher: Tell us why you think they belong together.

Skip: Because they are both stores and they both have meat in them.

David S.: What about Kathy's. It's a grocery store too.

Teacher: Now, Kathy? David suggested you move your picture over there, too. For what reason would he want you to put your picture in that group?

Kathy: They all have meat and milk and bread.

[35] Teacher: And——?

Kathy: That's what they were spending money for.

Sharon: Mine could go with Scott's.

Teacher: For what reason?

Sharon: He's getting pipes and mine's getting paint because our house is peeling.

[40] Scott: No! My dad is buying pipes for our cesspool.

Teacher: Can someone help us out? (pause)

Skip: The man has the paints and they sell them and they send out a man to paint the house and . . . (trails off)

Teacher: You're thinking, Skip, and that's good. Someone will get an idea. Yes, Laurie?

Laurie: mmmmmmmm. (very timidly)

[45] Teacher: All right, Laurie, come on.

Laurie: My picture could, could, could . . .

Teacher: What is your picture about?

Laurie: A carnival and clowns.

Teacher: And for what did your family spend money?

[50] Laurie: To go to the carnival.

Teacher: And with what other picture would you put your picture?

Laurie: I could put this by Kathy's because sometimes they have carnivals at the stores.

Teacher: All right, would you like to get your picture and put it with the stores? Boys and girls, did you hear what Laurie suggested? She would put her carnival by the stores because they have carnivals at the store sometimes. . . . Well, we still don't have a big idea about the pipes for the cesspool and the paint for the house. Let's let the question rest for a while and we'll start anew.

(to the video operator) Could we have a few minutes to stretch? . . . (pause in discussion)

Teacher: Let's see what we have done. These you have put together: the truck, the tractor, and the new automobile. And over here you have put together the flowers. And in these pictures you put together the house paint and the pipes for the cesspool. Over here you put all that sold meat, bread, and milk together with the carnival. Remember, Laurie wanted it there because they sometimes have carnivals at the stores. Now, for what purpose does your family spend its money? Who sees some other pictures that can be grouped together? Betty?

[55] Betty: Mitch's and Sue's.

Teacher: Why Mitch's and Sue's?

Betty: Because they're both buying clothes.

Teacher: Greg. I heard you say you wanted to put yours somewhere?

Greg: With Mitch's.

[60] Teacher: Why?

Greg: Because we're buying clothes, too.

David C.: My house can go with that one there.

Darrell: Mine.

Teacher: David, for what reason?

[65] David C.: Because they're both houses.

Teacher: Oh . . . but the question is, "For what reason did the family spend money?" Darrell, we never did listen to you tell about your interesting picture. . . .

Darrell: We're buying stuff.

Teacher: Wellll. . . . "Stuff" we can't use. Name it.

Darrell: Furniture.

[70] Teacher: What else?

Darrell: And our TV.

Teacher: David, did you hear Darrell explaining how his family spent their money? Can you find a reason for putting your picture with Darrell's?

David C.: We bought a TV too.

Teacher: All right, let's move your picture up here then. Does someone else see other pictures that could go together?

[75] Joel: Eric's should go with the car pictures.

Teacher: Joel, will you move Eric's over? Anything else that could go together?

David S.: Mine could go with Mitch's because his has a hill and so does mine.

Teacher: Oh, yes, but let's listen to the question. . . . "For what purpose did your family spend money?"

David S.: For our bridge.

[80] Teacher: Let's give it some more thought. We'll find a place for your picture, David. Greg?

Greg: I think the paint and the pipes could go together because they're both buying.

Children: No! Yes! No!

Teacher: Bring these two pictures over here. Let's take a look. The pipes are for Scott's cesspool and the paint is for Sharon's house because it's peeling.

David S.: And then they could go with my bridge because we're all fixing!

[85] Teacher: They are fixing. David has reached a big idea. David, would you like to bring your picture over here. Now, what shall I write above this group of pictures?

All: Fixing.

Kim: These pictures (trailers) could go with these because they are both stuff for the houses.

David S.: That isn't so! Bridges aren't for houses.

Teacher: Kim, this is a trailer. These are guns to go camping and this is another trailer.

[90] James: My dad's buying a new house. David's bridge and my house could go together because they're made of wood.

Teacher: That is one good reason for putting them together, James, but the question was "What did your family spend money for?"

James: Oh. Put it with Betty's and Diane's. They're all houses.

Teacher: Let's all think about this group with trailers and guns. Who can give me a big name that tells why these families spent money?

Child: Because they needed to go camping.

[95] Teacher: Why does a family go camping? Skip?

Skip: So they can relax for a little while.

Teacher: Oh, shall I put that down? These families spent money for relaxing. What a lovely word you used. . . . What shall I write above these pictures?

All: Relaxing.

Kim: I know what you can put together—store things and trailers because trailers should have food.

[100] Teacher: Yes, the families will need food, Kim, but we won't move the pictures right now. Greg, your people were buying shoes. Mitch, what were your people spending money for?

Mitch: Clothes.

Teacher: And Sue?

Sue: Dresses.

Teacher: What name shall we give this group? Greg?

[105] Greg: Buying clothes.

Teacher: All right, I'll write down "buying clothes". Now, let's see what we have here. Joyce, for what reason is Eric's family spending money?

Joyce: Ah. . . .

Teacher: Eric, do you want to tell Joyce what your parents are buying?

Eric: A new car.

[110] Teacher: Let's talk about these pictures of the new cars. For what purpose does a family buy a car?

Randy: So they can ride around and not have to walk everywhere. Like to the store.

Teacher: New cars are for——?

Child: Sale.

Teacher: (laughing) Yes, but, for what reason did the family spend money? Randy said so they wouldn't have to walk.

[115] Child: Riding.

Child: I was going to say if they didn't have a car, they couldn't go anywhere.

Teacher: Good. So new cars are for going——?

Children: Places.

Teacher: So now I'll write "going places" above the group. Let's look at this group of pictures. For what reason does a family buy plants?

[120] Skip: They keep the backyard clean. So call it "keeping backyards clean".

Teacher: Yes. For what reason does a family buy flowers? Craig?

Craig: To make your house pretty.

Teacher: What's another word for "pretty"?

Children: Nice, good, beautiful, clean.

[125] Teacher: Well, I'll put down that word from Michael—"beautiful".

Randy: Un-un. I said it.

Teacher: All right. "Beautiful" from Randy. We have over here a group of store pictures. For what purpose did the families spend money in these stores?

Child: For food.

Teacher: So I'll write "food" above these pictures. We still have Andy's picture.

[130] Child: I didn't know whose that was.

Child: What's it about?

Teacher: Andy, tell the boys and girls about your picture.

Andy: It's about buying furniture for my bedroom.

Teacher: Do you see a group where you would put your picture?

[135] Andy: With the house pictures because that's where furniture is.

Teacher: All right, Andy. You place it with that group. Now let's see the groups of pictures we'll put up to show some ways our families spend money. Here we have different cars we decided to call——?

Children: "Going places."

Teacher: And here——?

Children: "Houses."

[140] Teacher: We have different kinds of stores. We decided to call this one——?

Children: "Food."

Teacher: And here we have another kind of store——?

Children: "Clothes."

Teacher: And here we need money for——?

[145] Children: "Fixing."

Teacher: And here the families spend money to make things——?

Children: Nice, pretty, beautiful.

Teacher: It's a big word. I think Randy gave it to us. It's——?

Children: "Beautiful."

[150] Teacher: And here the people spend money for——?

Children: "Relaxing."

Teacher: All right, boys and girls, that's what we need to do now. You were very good to work so long. Thank you.

An observer pointed out that in the foregoing discussion the children really worked and worked hard. They reached into their own vocabularies to express the basic needs of man: shelter, food, clothes, transportation, maintenance, aesthetic satisfaction, and relaxation. But, the results of this discussion were really twofold. They included not only the expression of specific cognitive skills but also the building of self-image as each child was supported by his peers and recognized by name and contribution.

POINTS FOR THOUGHT

*Listing, Grouping, and Labeling**

1. The opening question should be broad enough to allow all children to respond. Each child present had drawn a picture.
   • What is the teacher's first question in entry [1]?
   • How does she adjust her question in entry [3]?
   • Why do they think she changed her wording?
2. The sampling should be broad and varied enough to provide an opportunity for students to form several groups. If the sampling is too narrow, the teacher must devise questions to get a broader sampling. After sixteen children had responded, the teacher felt she had an adequate sampling and that she should move to grouping.
3. Seven year olds generally group objects on a "concrete operational" level; some see relationships that are more abstract.
   • What reason does the teacher give the children for grouping the pictures in entry [7]?
   • List a grouping or two or more that the children have given under the following headings: Concrete-Operational (USES), More Abstract, and Mixed.
   • Reread the short sequence in entries [49]–[53]. How does the teacher handle Laurie's grouping?
   • Why do you suppose she handled it in this manner?

*See Chapter 9, page 94.

- Reread the "inappropriate" grouping suggested by David S. in entry [77]. How does the teacher handle David's contribution in entries [78] and [80]?
- Does the teacher's handling of David S.'s suggested grouping pay off later?
- Would you have handled either of these responses differently? If so, how?
- How many times does the teacher find it necessary to refocus as the children work on grouping?
- How often does a child give a reason for his grouping without being asked for it?

4. When a child expresses the relationship among items in a group by giving it a label, he has expressed another dimension of his thinking.
   - What question does the teacher use to move the children to labeling in entry [85]?
   - What additional questions does she ask to get labels in entries [93], [117], and [123]?
   - How does the teacher involve the children in the recap?

5. Concepts grow in complexity and in abstractness of definition. Such growth is seen in the concept of "market" in the two statements below:

   Grade 2—Goods are bought and sold in places called markets.
   Grade 7—Scarcity of manpower created a labor market.

   In comparing the two uses of the term "market", one sees the growing abstractness of the concept as it moves from identifying a place to a usage which implies it as the price for which the worker will sell his labor.

6. Growth in complexity of the concept of "interdependence" is apparent in these two generalizations:

   Grade 4—In many California industries, like the lumber industry, one worker depends on the other.
   Grade 6—People who lack one important resource are dependent on other countries for that resource. They trade their resources to meet their needs.

Without necessarily using the word, the students showed an understanding of interdependence between workers on the job, and of countries having and those needing important resources. The interdependence between countries lends itself to a further understanding of global political ties and exchange of ideas.

Strategies for Developing Inferences and Generalizations/Applying Generalizations

LEADING CHILDREN TO INFER AND TO GENERALIZE

ADEQUATE and relevant information must be gathered before a productive discussion can take place. The study questions the teacher provides for students should give the focus the teacher plans to use in discussion—such as comparing certain aspects of life in several different colonies (fifth grade) or among different Indian civilizations of precolonial Latin America (sixth grade). However, the intake of information should not limit the interests nor exploration of the students. The teacher should also make certain she directs the children's research to people as well as to places, events, and things.

Dr. Taba felt that students who did not have a "quick memory" tended to be left out of discussions. She commented, "I have never found a correlation between the struggle a student had trying to remember raw data and the level of his or her thinking." For this reason she insisted that the raw data the students had gathered be organized and highly visible to all before the class was asked to draw inference or to make generalizations. Do not wait until all the gathering of information on a general topic such as a colony or civilization is completed; rather, plan that specific topics, such as why people work, who does the work, and what is done with the product will be the next focus for discussion. Check each day with the committees, encourage them to inform another committee when they find information that it is looking for. Teachers found that having comparable material shared among committees during the same session made organizing it and recording it on the blackboard less time-consuming and the discussions shorter. Dr. Taba referred to any form of organization (timelines, murals, drawings, etc.) as retrieval charts; they are for all to use to help them remember the raw data they had read or heard. Most teachers waited until the day following the charting of materials to lead the discussion asking for inferences and generalizations.

To use this organized information for more than memory work, Dr. Taba and her colleagues developed a strategy called Developing Inferences and Generalizations. This strategy is a prelude to Applying Generalizations, a method reviewed in the second part of this chapter.

Inferring and Generalizing

The cognitive tasks of inferring and generalizing require the student to interpret, infer, and generalize about data. The strategy to teach these skills consists of asking the students the following questions, usually in the order found in Table 3.1.[3]

This pattern of inviting reasons to account for observed phenomena and generalizing beyond the data is repeated and expanded to include more and more aspects of the data and to reach more abstract generalizations.

TABLE 3.1.

Teacher	Student	Teacher
What did you notice? See? Find? Or what difference/likenesses do you notice (with reference to a particular focus)?	Gives items.	Makes sure items are accessible, for example: Chalkboard/chartpaper Transparency Individual list Pictures Item card Chooses item to pursue.
Why do you think this happened or how do you account for these differences?	Offers explanation which may be based on factual information and/or inferences.	Accepts. Seeks clarification if necessary.
What does this tell you about . . .?	Forms generalization.	Encourages variety of generalizations and seeks clarification where necessary.

[3] See Wallen, Norman E., Mary C. Durkin, Jack R. Fraenkel, Anthony McNaughton and Enoch I. Sawin. 1969. "Development of a Comprehensive Model for Social Studies for Grades One through Eight, Inclusive of Procedures for Implementation and Dissemination," *Final Report*, Project No. 5-1314, Washington, D.C.: U.S. Office of Education, October.

Teachers developed and used charts in a variety of ways:

Several seventh- and eighth-grade teachers used an overhead projector as students listed, grouped, and labeled their data. The teacher then duplicated a copy for each student to use in making inferences and generalizations.

Charts, timelines, etc., were updated throughout the study of a unit.

Teachers adapted their questioning to the ability of their students to search through the data before them. Strong fourth-grade students handled a question that asked them to search through the whole chart for likenesses and differences, while a sixth-grade class was asked to consider one item in the data on the Aztecs (farming) and then to find another piece of the data they thought might be related to it. In both cases the questioning worked.

Below you will note different sets of questions that might be used by sixth-grade teachers, both using a retrieval chart (Table 3.2), comparing the farming of the Maya, Aztec, and Inca cultures of pre-colonial Latin America.

The following lists illustrate questions based on Table 3.2 from two teachers.

Teacher A[4]

(*1*) Yesterday we talked about the different kinds of land these three tribes of Indians lived on. Now we are going to look at one way they used their land. Can you find one thing the farmers did in all three tribes? Can you find something else <u>all</u> these tribes did in their farming?

(*2*) What differences do you notice in the ways these different tribes farm?

(*3*) How do you account for this difference? (Zooming in on one difference at a time.) Add questions, if needed, to lead them to relate the information on land to the way farming is done.

(*4*) What idea does this give you about why the different tribes of Indians farmed as they did?

(*5*) Do you see anything else on the chart that might be related to farming? (Add questions if needed, to lead students to see the relation to religion.)

[4]These questions were planned for a class that had a very low reading level and history of poor achievement.

TABLE 3.2 Retrieval Chart.

	Maya	Aztec	Inca
Land	open forests early in highlands later in lowlands	grasslands	grasslands
	much wet land	much flat land in highlands	mountainous
		enough rain for land in growing season	flat land very high
			valleys
			much very dry land
Farming	cut trees	planted	planted
	burned dry trees	fertilized	fertilized
	planted	no irrigation	irrigated
	weeded	harvested	harvested
	no irrigation		terraced
	harvested		
	fallow		
Religion	many gods	war part of religion	worshipped "Creator of the Sun"
	late Mayans worshipped "Feathered Serpent" god of Toltecs	life after death	no temples (but palaces)
	human sacrifice	many festivals	some human sacrifice
	built temples	worshipped "Rain God" and "God of War"	life after death
		built temples	

(6) Tomorrow we will add some other information about activities of these people and see whether they relate to their beliefs.

Teacher B[5]

(1) I would like to have you look at the data we put on our chart about the farming our three tribes of Indians did before the Spaniards came. What likenesses or differences do you notice?

(2) How do you account for these differences? (Take several, one at a time.)

(3) How do you account for the likenesses?

(4) Is there any other data on the chart that seems to be related to farming?

(5) I would like to have each of you write a statement that would express an important idea about all these tribes.

Relating the Question Sequence to a Widely Accepted Idea of the Discipline

In the social study guides developed in Contra Costa County the main ideas are those generally agreed upon by sociologists (or anthropologists, etc.) as being important in the social sciences. The organizing idea is an aspect of the main idea that is expressed in more specific terms. The child should discover the idea in the data and express it in his own words.

The discussion using the information in Table 3.3 was a short sequence related to the ideas that follow.

(1) Main Idea: Interaction between people and their environment influences the way in which they meet their needs.

(2) Organizing Idea: Bedouin herders modify their behavior and their environment in order to make a living
- by moving herds to new pastures
- by selling animals and handmade things
- by buying necessities
- by weaving tents that absorb water
- by storing grain, digging wells
- by making tents open to the east, etc.

[5]These questions were planned for an academically strong but not considered gifted class.

TABLE 3.3.

The Desert Nomad Sells:	The Desert Nomad Buys:	The Desert Nomad Needs These People
camels goats rugs wool hides leather bags milk, cheese	cloth salt tobacco grain tea fruit coffee vegetables kerosene firearms pots and pans sewing machines flutes dates saddles	(Developed on day of recording) gun-maker metal worker sewing-machine maker farmer *(Following were added after caption changed to "Worker"): oil worker trader pottery worker leather worker

*Note from observer.

DISCUSSION SEQUENCE 1

People the Nomads Need

Class Description

Class of third-grade children. Most of the children read at grade level. According to the teacher not a "top" class but a bit better than average. The school is located in San Joaquin Valley surrounded by immense farms.

Materials

The first two columns of the retrieval chart (Table 3.3) had been developed by the children and teacher as the children gained information about trade between the nomad and the traders in the marketplace. This chart was on the wall in front of the children as the lesson progressed.

Focus of Lesson

The lesson attempted (1) to have students fill in the third column by examining the first two columns, and (2) to have the children formulate general statements from the information on the chart. This group had had no prior experience in *formulating generalizations.*

[1] Teacher: Yesterday you gave me this information for the chart. (Teacher points to the first two columns of the chart.) Let's look at it now for a couple of minutes and think of all the people, besides the trader, that the nomad needs . . . (pause). Debbie?

Debbie: A fireman who had a fire alarm.

Teacher: Who? Oh, the firearms. You're talking about the firearms. Jean, do you know what they call a person who makes firearms?

Jean: A fireman.

[5] Teacher: That's a good try. But that's not the way we use the word "fireman". Does anybody have an idea what we might call him?

Group: Chief, fireman. . . .

Teacher: What are firearms? Do you know what firearms are? Gary?

Gary: Firearms are ladders and things that you put out fires with.

Teacher: Maybe we need some help here. Let's clear this up. Chris?

[10] Chris: The farmer would need seeds. . . .

Teacher: Would you hold that for a moment, Chris. We're just a little bit mixed up on what firearms are.

Terry: I know, I know.

Teacher: Terry, could you help us?

Terry: Firearms are guns.

[15] Teacher: Guns. That is right. The kind of weapon that uses bullets and so on like guns. And you found out the nomad needed those to protect his herds.

Chris: Rifles.

Teacher: Now, I wonder who would make those. We want to put up here who makes those rifles.

Chris: Oh, a carpenter?

Teacher: No, a carpenter wouldn't make those. Maybe I should help you about this. Peter, do you want to say something?

[20] Peter: A blacksmith?

Teacher: That's sort of the kind of worker. Let's call him a gun-maker. Would that be OK?

Group: Yes, yea.

Peter: Guns are made out of metal. We could call him a metal-worker.

Teacher: Good thinking, Peter. We can list both names up here and you can use either one. Now there are some other kinds of workers we would need up here. Michelle?

[25] Michelle: We'd need somebody who makes the sewing machines.

Teacher: What shall we call that person?

Michelle: A man . . . a sewing machine maker.

After the session the teacher recalled that as she made the chart with the children they had offered "guns" and "rifles". Without thinking, she had written "firearms".

DISCUSSION SEQUENCE 2

Teacher: If the nomad must buy fruit, barley, and vegetables at the marketplace, what kind of person does he need?

Jessie: A wife?

[30] Teacher: To buy some things probably. Who would get these things to the market for him?

Dottie: A camel.

Teacher: Who. It takes a person who does much work first. If he's going to buy fruit, barley, and grain what kind of person does he need?

Jimmy: A butler?

Teacher: Well, he'd certainly be a rich person if he had a butler. Do you ever go to the store to buy a head of lettuce? . . . Did the lettuce grow there?

[35] All: A farmer!

DISCUSSION SEQUENCE 3

Teacher: Let's look at our chart for a moment. When we were making it yesterday you said the nomad sold sheep, goats, and camels. Did you mean he sold all of his animals?

All: No! He eats some. Saves some to have babies.

Teacher: Let's just talk about his flock of sheep. (The teacher moves to the chalkboard and makes a number of x's on the board.)

Let's pretend the family eats this part of the flock (erases a number of the crosses). We'll pretend these are the ones the nomad saves to have more lambs (draws a circle around them).

Now, what part does he sell?

Chris: The leg?

[40] Teacher: I think my question is too hard. We'll talk about this tomorrow.

The teacher said she was pushing for the word "remainder". She thought because they used it in subtraction they would use it here. Not so.

DISCUSSION SEQUENCE 4

Teacher: Let's look at the chart. Up in this last column I wrote "The Desert Nomad Needs These People". Maybe if we changed the word "People" to "Workers" it would help us. (Teacher crosses out "People" and writes "Workers". In quick succession the children added four more workers to their list and the teacher was ready to initiate the children into the skill of making generalizations.)

Teacher: I want you to look at the chart for a minute or two and think of something you could tell me about the nomads of the desert in one sentence.

Eddie: He rides on horses or camels or donkeys.

Teacher: All of these are . . .

[45] Eddie: Animals.

Teacher: Can you say that and just use the word "animals"?

Eddie: The nomad travels on animals. (Teacher quickly writes Eddie's contribution on board.)

Teacher: What else can we say about the desert nomads? Let's try not to name a list of things but do as Eddie did.

The teacher wrote each generalization quickly on the board as it was given.

Peter: They eat some dates, but not too many.

[50] Teacher: Is that all they do with them?

Peter: They feed the seeds to the camels.

Teacher: Could you say one thing that would tell me something about the nomad and the date?

Peter: The date is very useful to them.
Michelle: They take the wool and make the rugs.
[55] Teacher: Is that all they do with it?
Several: Nope. No.
Teacher: Let's let Michelle talk. They take the wool. They make——?
Michelle: The nomad takes wool and makes things.
Teacher: Fine. See how we learn from each other. Linda, do you have an idea you'd like to give us?
[60] Linda: They have different markets than we do.
Teacher: You said "different markets". You need a little bit more. I think. For instance, we might have Safeway in one spot here; and we might have Purity in another spot . . . (pause). Not just a different market but a different——?
Linda: A different kind of market.
Teacher: Good! A different kind of market. That's it. And you notice that when Linda said "kind", she sort of said it hard so I'll put a line under it. They have a different kind of market.
Chris: The nomad needs the oasis people and the oasis people need the nomad.
[65] Teacher: Thank you, Chris. That is a great idea. Rudy, do you have an idea about the nomads you'd like to share with us?
Rudy: The nomad buys more kinds of things than he sells.
Teacher: Good, Rudy, I'm glad you said "kind" the way you did because I think that's exactly what you're thinking. You have all done extremely well. We have six important ideas up here. I think you have done well for our first try. Thank you.

After the class discussion the principal relieved the teacher so she might talk to the observer about her first attempt at getting children to generalize. She said that she anticipated the first task (filling in the third column) would be a breeze for her students, so she didn't spend time on her focusing question. We all learned what havoc a vague question, a strange category, or a misleading question can cause. Even though the beginning was rocky, the children held on beautifully with the teacher on a beastly hot afternoon. The teacher chose to use the word "sentence" to lead the children to generalize because they were used to using it in spelling lessons. They understood it to be a statement.

POINTS FOR THOUGHT

*A Teacher's First Effort to Elicit Generalizations**

1. Looking at entry [1], check the focusing question the teacher asks. What wording do you think would have made the focus clearer to the children?
2. At what point does the teacher change the wording to make the focus clear?
3. Do you see a sequence in which the teacher's questions led the children away from the focus?

   What do you think the teacher had in mind?

   Why do you think the children were unable to come up with a reasonable response?
4. Note the teacher's question in entry [42] and how it is used to change the focus. Can the child respond to it?

   Now check the ways she asks the children to generalize in entries [52], [57], and [59].

   Note also that two children feel free to enter the discussion without being called on in entries [54] and [64].
5. Choose two generalizations that you feel are most powerful.

   a. _____

   b. _____

   Why did you choose these two?
6. Sharpening up the language. The opportunity to sharpen a child's English often occurs during class discussions. The teacher has to make the decision on her feet as to whether this particular child will benefit from such help and whether it can be done quickly without intruding on the flow-of-thought of the children. Note entries [60]–[63]. Linda's thinking is right in tune with the teacher's and the teacher does not have to repeat the focusing question. Chris [64] kept things moving without losing focus.
7. List any other problems you think might arise as you lead the class discussion.
8. Discuss with a partner or the group how these problems might be handled and record your suggestions.
9. Are there problems related to materials or the public that might cause concern?

*See Chapter 9, page 96.

POINTS FOR THOUGHT

Formulating Questions**

1. You are a teacher of seventh-grade social studies. The content studied has focused on the cultural achievements of Egypt, Greece, and Rome. The students have studied Phoenician traders, the Roman Republic, Judaism, Alexander the Great, the Roman Empire, Christianity, the Roman Army, Islam, Egyptian beliefs, and Roman beliefs.

   You feel the students have enough information to be able to discover the relationship between the spread of ideas and achievements through trade, invasion, and other contacts while some ideas and achievements are rejected or changed. You ask:
   - What did Egyptians believe, know, or invent? (List on the chalkboard, as in Figure 3.1.)
   - Which of the ideas or inventions you listed for Egypt were found also in Greece? (Extend to a second list for Greece by means of arrows, as in Figure 3.1.)
   - What other ideas or invention should we add to the Greek list?
   - Do the same for Rome in a third list.

   Now add the questions you would ask to elicit from the

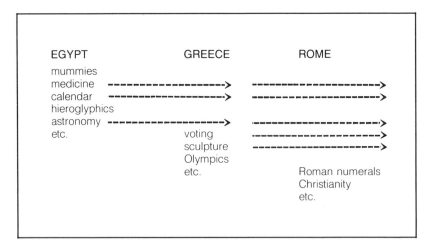

Figure 3.1.

**See Chapter 9, page 98.

students statements that are both logical and relevant. You may wish to work with a partner in planning the question sequence.

APPLYING GENERALIZATIONS TO NEW SITUATIONS

One of the best evaluation techniques for testing how well students understand the generalizations they have developed, is to show they recognize a new situation as one to which a formerly learned generalization might apply. The task encourages students to support their speculations with evidence and sound reasoning.

The first step is for students to make inferences, for example, in response to a question such as: "What would happen to the way of life in the desert if the government helped all the farmers of the oasis buy tractors?"

The second step is that of explaining or supporting the inference by linking the condition (loss of the camel market) and the inference. For example, if a third-grade student infers, "If they can't sell their camels, they'll build towns," the teacher needs to help him make explicit the chain of causal links that lead from the loss of the camel market to the building of the towns.

Figure 3.2 illustrates one third grade's causal continuum. Applying generalizations to new situations invites a greater degree of divergent thinking than does either of the two previously described cognitive tasks. Unless the teacher is aware of the multiple possibilities, it is easy to limit the discussion to the most obvious suggestions. On the other hand, the divergence can be carried to the point of sheer fantasy. It is, therefore, equally important for the teacher to see to it that the students are challenged to produce factual and logical support for their inferences. To assist teachers in leading students to discover whether generalizations they have made in one situation are applicable in another, Dr. Taba and her colleagues developed a strategy called Applying Generalizations.

APPLYING GENERALIZATIONS[6]

To apply generalizations consists of using previously learned generalizations and facts to explain unfamiliar phenomena or to infer conse-

[6]Wallen et al. 1969. *Final Report*, p. 19.

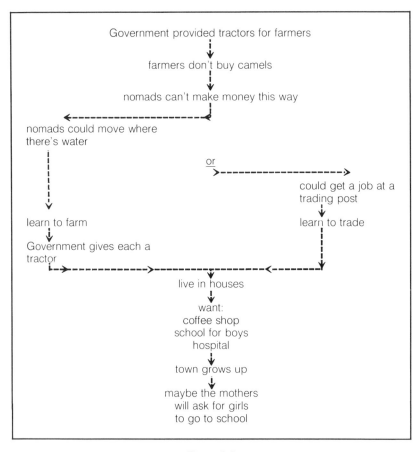

Figure 3.2.

quences from known conditions. It encourages students to support their speculations with evidence and sound reasoning. The teaching strategy consists of asking in order the questions found in Table 3.4.

This pattern of inviting inferences, requiring explanations, identifying necessary conditions, and encouraging divergent views is continued until the teacher decides to terminate the activity.

DISCUSSION SEQUENCE

What Would Happen If . . . ?

Class Description

Class of about thirty sixth graders. The school is located in a suburb of modest homes and modest incomes. The group is considered academically strong but not gifted.

Materials

A chart developed by teacher and students contained information on the resources, exports, standard of living, etc., of Argentina. This chart was in easy view for all the students as the discussion took place.

Focus

The students had previously studied the effects of a severe freeze on Brazil's coffee crop and the effect of the loss of their export market on the economy. The teacher's focus was to see whether the class would

TABLE 3.4.

Teacher	Student	Teacher Follow-Through
(Focusing question) Suppose that (a particular event occurred given certain conditions), what do you think would happen?	Makes inference.	Encourages additional inferences. Selects inference to develop.
What makes you think that would happen?	States explanation; identifies relationships.	Accepts explanation and seeks clarification if necessary.
What would be needed for that to happen?	Identifies conditions necessary to a particular inference.	Decides whether these conditions are sufficient and are likely to be present in the given situation.
(Encouraging diversity) Can someone give a different idea about what would happen?	States new inferences that differ in some respects from preceding ones.	Encourages alternative inferences, requests explanations and necessary conditions. Seeks clarification where necessary.
If, as one of you predicted, such-and-such happened, what do you think would happen after that?	Makes inferences following from the given inference.	Encourages additional inferences and selects those to pursue further.

spontaneously recall any likenesses or differences between Brazil's crisis and the situation given below.

[1] Teacher: If 80 percent of Argentina's exports is beef at the present time, and the cattle suddenly become infected with a disease that would prohibit meat being exported, what do you think would happen?

John: Well . . . they just have to grow more wheat 'cause they have to have money to run the country and feed the people who will be out of work.

Teacher: All right, John, you say they'll grow more wheat.

Carol: Well, I disagree with John because when you're trying to grow a crop like that—you could grow wheat or another crop, sure. But it takes money to get irrigated, if you have to get irrigated. It takes money to get the education you need for farming and you don't have enough money left over from something when you go bankrupt. You've put all your money in the cattle industry, the cattle industry goes down, you're out.

And as far as the wheat goes, well, sure you can switch to wheat, but you're not going to get half as much money. The price would probably go down, 'cause there'll be more of it.

[5] Teacher: Well, we've got some real problems, if we agree with this.

Charles: Well, you can be sure that there will be stock in the meat industry, right? I mean stock like the stock market. Some millionaire man, he has stock in the meat industry, all his money put into this instead of the other corporations. But he has most of it in the cattle stock market, so then other countries stop buying the cattle or meat from their country and they don't have any buyers. So the stock market goes down, and these millionaires would go down. I mean they would just go broke!

Teacher: Then you are saying people should have invested in other corporations as well as cattle?

Charles: Yes, then they wouldn't lose everything.

Teacher: Carol thinks there would be additional problems if Argentina increased the growth of wheat. What other way of getting money can you suggest for Argentina?

[10] Cindy: Well, like when Brazil had that terrible freeze and it killed coffee trees, they had to have money to buy things they had to have.

Teacher: Such as?

Cindy: I'd say to borrow money to get machines for their factories and to build factories to make machinery. Seems nobody down there makes big machinery for factories. Everyone imports them. They cost more that way.

Teacher: What could Argentina do with the money they save?

Cindy: They could buy a lot of materials to make factories.

[15] Josh: They already make a lot of machinery.

Cindy: But most of it is used for crops and like Carol said they're already producing too much wheat, corn, and beef.

Teacher: Oh, they're not industrial machines? They're not factory machines? Charles?

Charles: Well, yes, some, like, for processing wheat into cereal, but not the kind for minerals and ore. The problem is Argentina, they have rich minerals, but just don't have men or machines and equipment to work on it and reach it.

Teacher: Where will they get the money to buy machines and equipment? Jean?

[20] Jean: Borrow money from the United States.

Teacher: You suggest borrowing from the United States. What if the United States is not willing to loan the money?

Jean: They'll borrow it from somebody else.

Sylvia: Well, I know that Argentina, once it does have machinery— even if they get the machines, they'd have to get the fuel to run them. They don't have hardly any fuel. So I'd like to know how they'd solve that problem after they got the machines.

Teacher: Has Argentina been working on this problem?

[25] Nancy: Yes. Argentina's government has been trying to—they are trying but it's hard because they don't have large supplies of good coal and iron. They're trying to encourage industry, and trying to build dams on the Colorado River, just like the one they done on the Negro River.

Teacher: And how does this help?

Nancy: They could run the machines with electricity.

Teacher: Instead of . . .

Nancy: Oil or coal.

[30] Teacher: Good, Nancy. Can anyone tell me just what advantage Argentina finds in developing industries? Ben?

Ben: Well, more people could get a job, more people could work, and you have more money. Like in Brazil. When they started making cars lots of people left little farms or raising cattle and started making cars. People buy the cars and you have surplus money to buy extra tools and then you sell more and get more money. Just like that.

Teacher: Very clearly stated, Ben. Thank you. Does anyone have something to add to that? Jeff?

Jeff: We've been talking about getting machines and do more mining but you've gotta have men, too, and no one wants to work in the mines. And that's not just Argentina. We found out Costa Rica has the same problem. Argentina doesn't have a large enough labor force; they only have three out of a hundred people. Ninety-seven percent are white and 90 percent are educated, and they're all working good jobs like policeman or something like that, and they don't have the labor force for mining or anything like that. Argentina has a big middle class.

Teacher: Since you used the term "middle class" we'd better make sure everyone understands what you mean by "middle class".

[35] Jeff: Well, they're not too poor, they don't live in the slums or anything like that, they are not too rich, they don't live up in big mansions or anything like that. They just live in sort of a middle place.

Teacher: Would someone like to add to Jeff's explanation?

Cody: Well, they have a fine education and they do not need to scrounge for work, they have jobs offered to them. Instead, the lower-class people — and I'm not saying where and in some of ours — they have to ask for work, beg from people, and then take real low wages, and your very rich people, you have so many rich people, they'll just be wanting people to work for lower wages.

Teacher: Could it be an advantage for a country to have a very large middle-class working force?

Tonia: Well, it's definitely an advantage because I know, in the United States, well, almost everybody in the United States is a middle-class worker. And the United States is a very rich country, then it's bound to have an advantage.

[40] Teacher: Shall we list this as an additional problem that Argentina faces in developing mines and factories? It's worth our doing some study about the problem. Does Brazil have the same problem?

Child: No. Brazil has lots of lower-class people who work in the mines, but some don't even have jobs.

Carol: Maybe Argentina could develop their tourist trade more. I read that Haiti used to have a big tourist attraction but it deteriorated. Now they are trying to raise that attraction so they can have as many tourists as they used to have.

Teacher: That's another idea. Good. Any more ideas? Charles?

Charles: Well, so many countries in Latin America have one problem, and that is industry, but none of them has thought of inviting other corporations from other countries and maybe they'll think of a lot of things to do. And educate the people. They need work.

[45] Teacher: A fine idea, Charles. And I'm happy that so many of you realize that it's the working-class people that need the education and the industry to work in. Let's look at the suggestions we've charted on the board (see Figure 3.3). Would you say Brazil's loss of the coffee market and Argentina's loss of the cattle and processed meat market were the same? Could both countries' problems be solved in the same way? Wendy?

Wendy: Well, it seems that every country in all of Latin America needs to—or almost everyone needs a better education and more machinery. So if Brazil and some workers in Argentina can get that, well, it seems most of their problems would be ended.

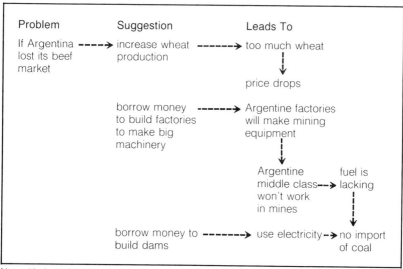

Note: Horizontal arrows (→) indicate consequences of actions; vertical arrows (↓) indicate negative arguments.

Figure 3.3.

Teacher: Bev, did you want to say something?

Bev: Up there on the board you wrote "big middle class". If Argentina wants to have a lot of mines like Brazil there'll be trouble getting workers. I don't think Brazil had trouble because they already do a lot of mining.

Jeff: Well, Argentina should go for factories—like Brazil's car industry. You can build factories where you think is a good spot but you sure can't move a mine. They need money, but it's hard to get.

[50] Teacher: Thank you for your good ideas. I'm certain these countries feel they have many problems in common and at the same time there are important differences among them that must be considered.

Figure 3.3 depicts the chart the teacher referred to near the close of the foregoing discussion [45]. Two students recorded the suggestions as they were made. Students were familiar with this style of diagramming.

POINTS FOR THOUGHT

What Would Happen If . . . ?†

Reread the complete discussion sequence "What Would Happen If . . .? before answering the questions that follow.

1. The focus states the teacher plans to check whether the students will make a spontaneous comparison between two situations that seem similar. How many students speak before a comparison is made? Is the comparison made spontaneously or does the teacher give a leading question?
2. Reread the teacher's question in entry [7] and the response in entry [8]. What comment would you make about that teacher/student sequence?
3. Can you think of a better question to have asked following the response in entry [6]?
4. Reread the response in entry [42]. Why might the teacher not have pursued the differences and likenesses between Argentina and Haiti?

†See Chapter 9, page 99.

5. Reread Tonia's statement in entry [39]. What inaccuracy do you note? How would you have dealt with Tonia's inaccuracy?

DISCUSSION SEQUENCE

Why Wouldn't It Happen?

In a fourth-grade class discussion of the effects of the Gold Rush of 1849 on the Sierra, the class developed a chain of events. The teacher planned a second discussion that would give the class an opportunity to consider whether similar events might be expected in what might appear to be a similar situation. The diagram in Figure 3.4 was used as a retrieval source in the second discussion.

Mr. B.: Suppose oil is discovered on the Harris Ranch, what do you suppose would happen?

Anna: People would rush in to work here.

Leroy: Yeah, and they would start building dance halls.

J. B.: No more tomatoes because it's just like those people who jumped ship in San Francisco and came to mine gold. Those field-workers will want to work in oil. Bet it pays more.

Mr. B.: Yes, Anna. Do you want to add more?

```
gold discovered → word gets out → miners come → need tools →
                                                  food
                                                  clothes
                                                  tents
                                                  etc.

people come to set up stores → wives and children come →
                               cook, do
                               hard work

need homes → people want entertainment → build dance halls →
schools                                   show houses
teachers

people fight → government set up → build jails
                                   town grows up
```

Figure 3.4.

Anna: I want to disagree with Leroy and J. B. and myself. It wouldn't be like that—people aren't going to run around with tin pans or cups dipping up oil. They don't do it that way. Once in a while someone drives a pickup out there where the pumps are and I guess he just checks things.

Mr. B.: Anna, you've been thinking things over. That's good. But before we go on I'd like to have you clear up something you said. You mentioned the people running around with tin pans. Is that the only way the miners got the gold from the earth?

Anna & others: Nooo! Big mines, little mines, just dug into the hill, hosing the stream banks.

Mr. B.: Okay. Now let's think about what Anna has just said about the drilling of oil.

POINTS FOR THOUGHT

Why Wouldn't It Happen?††

1. Plan a sequence of questions that would help the students draw on their life experience to point out some of the many conditions that differ from the days of the Gold Rush. (Oil had been discovered on a farm not two miles from the school. It was judged to be a small deposit. Only one well was drilled. It had been operating four or five years in the melon patch.)

††See Chapter 9, page 99.

CHAPTER 4

Yardsticks for the Classroom Teacher

LEVELS OF THOUGHT AND CUE WORDS

TEACHERS participating with the research team in their evaluation of progress in cognitive skills requested yardsticks by which they might judge a child's speech or writing quickly and easily. Probably most teachers would consider those listed in Figure 4.1 as the easiest to apply when checking a lift in a child's thinking.

Cue Words

For those who wish to sharpen their ears a bit more, "cue words" are suggested. In his paper Dr. McNaughton remarks that Oliver, Shaver, Taba, and Fenton agree on the value of students expressing the tentative and probabilistic character of knowledge.[7]

The research team suggested words or phrases teachers might listen for as cues to qualities of thinking, and to which their ears might quickly become attuned. A number of such qualities and the words that are evidence for them are presented in the following sections.

Tentativeness/Probability

Words or phrases that indicate tentativeness are *probably; it seems as if; but; the evidence suggests that,* etc. Example: "They (elders) would probably want to stick to the way that their ancestors did it." (third grader)

[7]McNaughton, A. H. 1969. "A Generalization Is a Generalization," *The Record Teacher College,* 70:8.

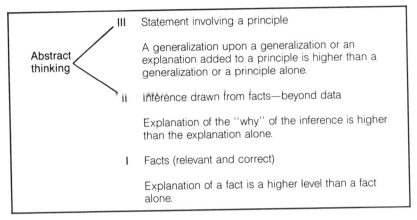

III Statement involving a principle

Abstract thinking

A generalization upon a generalization or an explanation added to a principle is higher than a generalization or a principle alone.

II Inference drawn from facts—beyond data

Explanation of the "why" of the inference is higher than the explanation alone.

I Facts (relevant and correct)

Explanation of a fact is a higher level than a fact alone.

Figure 4.1 Levels of thought.

Precision

Precision is achieved by subordinate clauses, phrases, or infinitives. For example, subordinate clauses are introduced by the words *who, which,* or *that.* Example: "Countries that lack an important resource depend on countries that have that resource" (sixth grader). Phrases use words such as *in, if, by, although,* and *yet.* Example: "Workers in modern industries depend on each other to get the job done" (fourth grader). Infinitives using *to* suggest students are offering a cause or reason, as in, "They went to the field *to pull* weeds," instead of "*and pulled* weeds". Or "My dad bought stuff *to take* up in the mountains *to work* on a bridge at my grandma's house." (first grader)

Comparison

Comparison is achieved by explaining a generalization regarding a person or situation being made with another generalization regarding a person or situation using such words as *different from, similar to, compared with,* etc. Example: "Problems that trouble many people often require a different level of government to deal with the problems, like when the United States changed from farms to industry, the government began to deal with many new problems." (eighth grader)

Inclusive or Abstract Words

Using words such as *equipment* rather than naming a series of articles suggests the student is thinking of a set or class. Those generalizations are best that have the most inclusive or abstract concept words in them so long as all words are relevant and not copied from the source of data.

POINTS FOR THOUGHT

Evaluating Students' Generalizations*

1. Examine the generalizations below. Mark (+) the four you consider the highest generalizations and (−) the four you consider the lowest. Be prepared to explain why.
Rating
   1. The exports are agricultural products or ores.
   2. Probably the low literacy results in a lack of skills, and that's why they don't process their raw materials.
   3. Brazil has the most people.
   4. The major industry of a people would probably influence the type of import and export.
   5. Except for one country, the capitals are also the largest cities while in our country that isn't true.
   6. Generally, it seems people tend to speak the language of the people who colonize the country.
   7. Generally, unless there's more we don't know about, your ancestry will determine how good your chance is for an education.
   8. The father is the head of the family in all the countries except Haiti.
   9. Most of the people are working in agriculture so that's why they import so much machinery.
   10. The Indians still speak their Indian language.
   11. The isolated people have retained their own language.
   12. Those countries that sell the most to the United States also buy the most from the United States.

*See Chapter 9, page 100.

CHAPTER 5

Self-Evaluation and Autonomous Thinking

LETTING STUDENTS "IN ON" THE CRITERIA OF EVALUATION

SINCE one of the goals of the Taba curriculum is to encourage students to become autonomous in their thinking, we need to consider how we can help them become critical of the products of their own thinking. To the degree maturity permits, a student should be encouraged to discover the criteria by which his/her thinking is being evaluated, judge the reasonableness of the criteria, and become self-critical in judging inferences, generalizations, and predictions he/she makes. The student's insights need not be limited to an understanding of why a teacher asks a particular question, such as "What would be necessary in order for this to happen?", but should also include an understanding of what is gained when many small groups exchange information or when a person organizes a large volume of information before trying to generalize from it.

Evaluation by students need not be conducted in separate, formal sessions. Rather, experience indicated that students' evaluation is more effective and less tedious when it is frequent and informal. Students need frequent opportunities to focus on the strength or weakness of their generalizations or to examine the way they have used a particular chart.

DISCUSSION SEQUENCE

Improving Statements Made by Students[8]

Class Description

The class had an enrollment of thirty-two fourth graders, and the

[8]Much of the content for this section has been taken with permission from Taba, Hilda, Mary C. Durkin, Jack R. Fraenkel and Anthony H. McNaughton. 1971. *A Teacher's Handbook to Elementary Social Studies.* Reading, MA: Addison-Wesley Publishing Co.

43

school was located in a modest middle-class neighborhood of Contra Costa County of California. There was a considerable range of academic ability but no students who tested as gifted. This class seemed above average in human relations—always helping each other and expecting to help. Rarely was there any dissension.

Material

A retrieval chart developed during the study of California history and geography was hanging in view of all the children during the discussion. In addition, the teacher had written on the board a statement given by a student the previous day.

Focus

The discussion was planned to focus on two statements made by students. Each was selected to provide opportunities for the class to recognize features that were good and those that could be improved. The class had previously performed this task a number of times immediately after a student had given a generalization, or when the teacher invented a sample.

[1] **Teacher:** I have written on the board a statement that Michael made yesterday. It's good for us to take time to look back over statements and see what we can learn from them. I want you to look for good things and things we can improve. Kevin, will you read Michael's statement.
Kevin: "Our state produces a variety of food because we have the topography, climate, water, and soils to grow things."
Child: He's telling how come we produce a variety of things—we—because we have better things to grow them in . . .
Teacher: When someone tells "why" we usually say——? Diana?
[5] **Diana:** He gave a reason.
Teacher: Does anyone see something we could improve? Peggy?
Peggy: Well, instead of listing them—topography, climate, water, and soil—you could say "We have the things to grow them."
Teacher: Can anyone think of another name for the group when we put them together? . . . (long pause). This is hard to pull together. Sometimes it's hard to remember a word that we actually know. Michael?
Michael: Wellll . . . you have all that grows and things that grow them.

[10] Teacher: Do you think "things" is a good way to say it? Could you be more <u>definite</u> than just "things"?

Michael: Yeah. Gee, it's soil and water and climate and topography.

Teacher: Well, we'd be listing again, wouldn't we? Diana?

Diana: Is it materials to grow them?

Teacher: Is climate a material?

[15] Diana: No, but it's used to grow . . .

Michael: It's what you have to have to grow something. I keep thinking of oranges and cotton.

Teacher: Michael, "things" is a possibility. There's nothing wrong with it. There's a word that is quite useful in many situations and I think many of the class really know it. David?

David: Products. Try "products".

Teacher: Are these products: topography, climate, soil, and water?

[20] David: No.

Teacher: Lorrie.

Lorrie: Natural resources?

Teacher: Are these natural resources, Lorrie?

Lorrie: Climate is a natural resource. Like if people come some place in the winter because they like the climate. You get a tourist industry. And they make movies where there are a lot of sunny days.

[25] Teacher: Lorrie, you have given us a good line of thinking. Lorrie has mentioned a couple of situations that have to have "things" just right. You all understand that each crop has to have just the right climate, soil, water, and quite often, topography. The word I'm thinking of is "conditions".

Several: Oh! Road conditions! They're always talking about "skiing conditions" on the radio.

Teacher: I was certain you had heard that word many times. Think for a moment about the conditions cotton needs to grow here in California . . . (pause). What did you think of? Michelle.

Michelle: Hot weather, water they get from irrigation, right soil, and level land.

Teacher: Can you think of a crop grown in California where at least one condition would have to be different?

[30] Lorrie: Strawberries. They like the fog and not so hot.

Teacher: Now, we're ready to go back to Michael's statement. He started the statement with a particularly good word. Jeff.

Jeff: Variety.

Teacher: Good. Mike, how would you like your statement to read now?

Mike: We produce a variety of foods because California has lots of different conditions these foods need.

[35] Teacher: Thank you, Michael. Your statement gives us a reason for the first part of your statement, we pulled some things together and your classmates did some good thinking with you. I have another statement I should like to have you look at. Steven, will you read it out loud.

Steven: "Workers depend on each other."

Teacher: Now this is correct for the workers we have been studying about lately, but our chart has more information on it. Think back to people you have studied about earlier this year. Look at the information on the chart. Would this statement be true for them? Bruce.

Bruce: Well, the Indians. They depended on nature, but if they need a house, or food they built their own house and hunted or gathered their food.

Teacher: Did they have a system where each had a part of a job then passes the job along to another? Judith.

[40] Judith: No. They did the whole job.

Teacher: All right. Jean, you gave us this statement yesterday and it is true. Now we've talked a little more about workers. What would you say now?

Jean: We could say some workers depend on each other.

Teacher: Yes, and that would be right. Would we know which people these were?

David: Modern day workers depend on each other.

[45] Teacher: Now David, go on and add what Bruce said.

David: I've forgotten what Bruce said.

Teacher: David has helped Jean with the first part. Who can add to what Bruce was saying? Mandy?

Mandy: Modern workers depend on each other to do a job, but the Indians didn't depend on anyone but themselves.

Judith: That's not right. When the mission people came they helped each other. They depended on each other.

[50] Teacher: This is true, Judith. You have made a very important point. That's when things changed, isn't it? This is when the California Indians started doing special jobs. I'm glad you brought that up, because there's another important point to make. Some Indians did divide their labor into special jobs. You will study about them in the sixth grade. Judith, how do you think we could say this so it will explain which people Jean was thinking of and give us Bruce's idea.

Judith: We could say, "Workers in modern industry depend on each other, but in early times some people did not divide up the work into special jobs.

Teacher: I think all of you have done a good job working on these statements. To end the discussion, could we say some things that are important when we are making big statements. What are some of the things we did this morning? Jeff.

Jeff: Like, say topography and climate—put all of them together in just one word.

Teacher: What else? David.

[55] David: Comparing. Like when we were talking about modern workers and workers of earlier times.

Teacher: Yes. But remember Jean's statement was correct the way she had stated it.

Jean: We improved it.

Teacher: How did we improve your statement?

Jean: By explaining more.

[60] Teacher: Judith, is there anything more we did?

Judith: We helped each other.

Teacher: In what way?

Judith: Like someone would start a sentence and someone else would add to it.

Teacher: Cynthia.

[65] Cynthia: We showed reasons why.

Lorrie: We discussed a word and if you really know what it means and if it's really true.

Teacher: These are all important things to remember. One more thing that's important—what are we doing when we say "from what we know—from what we have learned"? Michael.

Michael: That's just what we mean—that it's like umm we only had learned about one part of the world or only a bit about something.

Teacher: So what are we telling ourselves?

[70] Michael: We don't know it all; just part of it.

Teacher: Good. Thank all of you.

POINTS FOR THOUGHT

*Improving Statements Made by Students**

Reread the complete discussion sequence, Improving Statements Made by Students before answering the questions below.

1. The teacher [8] asks "What do you want to call (four items) when they're put together?" At what point does he/she give the word he/she has in mind? _____

   In entry [17] the teacher seems certain the students know the word that could name the group. If the students know the word, then the teacher is asking them to perform what mental function?

   _____

   If you feel the name of the group should have been given earlier, at what point would you have given it? _____

   Why at that point? _____

   _____

2. Beginning with entry [53] examine the list of "yardsticks" the students give. How do they compare with the list given by Dr. Taba and the research team?

3. Reread the passage [33] to [46] on pp. 34–35 and indicate: (1) the desirable qualities of thinking found in speakers [33], [37], and [46], and (2) whether the qualities appear spontaneous.

   [33] Jeff: _____

   _____

   [37] Cody: What do you think he might be trying to avoid saying? _____

   Why do you think he would avoid saying more?

   _____

   _____

   [46] Wendy: _____

Examples of teacher eliciting an improved response: All the countries? All the people?, etc.?, Can you make a statement that sums up——?, Can you think of another situation that was similar?, etc.

*See Chapter 9, page 101.

CHAPTER 6

Are Poor Readers Also Poor Thinkers?

INTAKE OF INFORMATION WITH EMPHASIS ON THE POOR READER

DR. Taba recognized the problems of teacher and student when the student is a poor reader. She urged teachers to draw from life experiences when appropriate, to use study trips, and to teach all students to "read" every type of media.

No student can raise his level of thinking without adequate intake of information. Because every teacher is faced with students who learn in a variety of ways, there are certain questions she must ask herself as she formulates study questions that give focus to the gathering of information.

Questions on Information Sources

(1) *Multimedia:* Is the content of my study question discoverable in more than one medium?

(2) *Available for re-use:* Is content available in a form that I may use more than once with students who will benefit from consuming their intake in smaller bites? (Remember, films are usually scheduled very tightly.)

(3) *Taping outside resource persons:* Is the person I plan to use as a resource willing to be videotaped? (Resource persons often give too much information for a class to absorb in one sitting.)

(4) *Guidance to resource:* Have I given some guidance to the resource person as to the information we need?

(5) *Study prints:* Are the available study prints just pretty pictures or do they provide the information I want the students to get? (For instance, if you are trying to teach a process, such as lumbering in California, flow-pictures are necessary rather than just pictures of trees.)

(6) *Listening posts:* Can some of the content be made available at the listening posts? (For instance, teachers could select really meaty sections from a book, and then rewrite and tape them. Think of what it does for the self-concept of the child who can then report information others do not know.)

(7) *Files:* Do my files contain appropriate pictures or articles I can use? (One sixth-grade teacher of a very low-achieving class arranged with the homeroom mother to organize a group to mount the many materials she had in her files. The school's audio-visual department provided mounting material and advice. The teacher then had several boxes of source materials easily and quickly available to all students.

(8) *Handbooks, yearbooks, charts:* Are these materials accessible? Teachers who spent time teaching the total class the efficiency of looking up data in well-charted books, such as almanacs, handbooks, and yearbooks on countries being studied reported all students liked to get raw data from them. (One young teacher started the teachers on this track when she noted her own fourth-grade brother checking the annual baseball records of his favorites.)

(9) *Interviews:* Can I make use of interviews? Interviewing is another source of information. Give the children training and guidelines for interviewing. In a first-grade class studying "where children learn", the children asked such questions of parents and grandparents, as "When did you learn about heroes?", and "Who told you about him/her?" This led to another dimension of the idea as parents or grandparents told of different heroes in the different countries from which they had come; this is one way of introducing the continuity of family and community. Parents should be let in on what you are trying to do so they won't say "I think it would be better if you would go look it up."

(10) *Read to students:* Am I reluctant to read to students? Do not apologize for reading to your students. Students of all ages like to be read to. Make certain the material is worth your time.

(11) *Questions on people:* Do my study questions contain questions about people and their feelings? Social studies is not all raw data and map skills, and levels of thinking, but, most importantly, it is people and their ways of dealing with their resources.

(12) *Opening new doors:* Do my questions open the door to a new world for these children? Pursue such questions as "How did the

writer get this information?" Through such questions they learn of the work of such professionals as anthropologists and sociologists.

(*13*) *Sharing information:* Do I encourage children to learn from each other? Some teachers at the end of a study period would ask a question such as, "Do we have an example of one committee finding an answer for another committee having difficulty finding information?" Children were very helpful in reporting the needed information, or where it could be found. Teachers also had students read to their committees, and had students report what they had listened to at the listening posts, etc.

(*14*) *Texts and tradebooks:* Can I use resource persons more meaningfully? Texts are usually shallow in dealing with people. They rarely offer a picture of the whimsy or humor of mankind. Here is where the librarian can oe of great help. But she/he must know just what you are searching for.

(*15*) *Teamwork to support a process curriculum:* Do I help identify the materials that support inductive teaching? It is not unusual for teachers within a school to share social studies books on the basis of geographical area being studied. Thus Mr. X teaches colonial Pennsylvania and Ms. Z teaches colonial Massachusetts. Then the teachers switch books. If a school district decides to construct a curriculum that emphasizes thinking skills, comparing and contrasting the content studied becomes an important aspect of its teaching. Such organization of curriculum could require access to adequate materials by the three teachers at approximately the same time. Teachers, audio-visual specialists, and curriculum developers should cooperate in determining which films are the best teaching materials, and hence should be purchased in quantity.

DISCUSSION SEQUENCE

Good Thinking from the "Wrong Side of the Room"

Is a social studies curriculum that attempts not only to teach the content but to lift the level of children's thinking workable with children who are not reading at grade level? Dr. Taba felt strongly that if we provided a variety of ways of presenting the necessary information to the children we would find many "poor readers" to be "good thinkers".

Class Description

The class consisted of third-grade children from an economically deprived area of Contra Costa County. Most of the children had language and reading problems. They were seated according to their reading group.

Focus of Discussion

The class was studying a tribal society. During approximately thirty minutes of discussion, the changes and the agents of change had been listed as follows on the chalkboard:

Changes	People Who Brought Change
Metal tools	Peace Corps
Metal pans	Missionaries
Medicine	Traders
Nurses	Travelers
Schools	World Health Organization
Books	
Bicycles	
Bigger Buildings	

The teacher then moved beyond the data and the following sequence took place.

[1] Teacher: Do you think these people would have discovered these things all by themselves some day without the help of these other groups coming with new ideas?

Margie: No.

Teacher: What do you think—how would it be if these people hadn't come?

Margie: Well, they'd still be living in their old ways—for instance their houses—until they just got so old, centuries and centuries. And maybe some day they'd find out about these ways and these things.

[5] June: Maybe they would find out about our ideas—like if one person from the village traveled around to the cities in Africa or America and then came back to his village and traveled all around and spread it and told them. Maybe some wouldn't believe it.

Teacher: How could he help them to believe what he saw?

June: Tell them or take a picture or something.

Margie: Or he could do it himself and start building that kind of building.

Teacher: Start building better buildings after what—after what he had seen?

[10] Margie: If he wanted to, he could show them how they did it.

Mike: Some people wouldn't believe it unless they went over there, because almost all people believe that they already have everything. I mean, I mean if the African from that little village came back and told the natives, they probably wouldn't believe it.

The next response was made by a little boy named Ryan who stammers and has many problems in the classroom.

Ryan: Yes, I think they would learn by themselves. If they couldn't learn what we have, how come they learned what they are already doing?

Teacher: (with a shocked look on her face) Say that once more.

Ryan: If they can't learn what we have here, how can they learn what they have already learned there?

[15] Teacher: They have already learned by themselves. You think they would teach themselves new ideas?

Ryan: That's right.

After the discussion was concluded, the teacher remarked, "The good answers were coming from the 'wrong side' of the room."

POINTS FOR THOUGHT

*Success When the Poor Reader Is Invited to Think**

After you have read the total discussion sequence, reread the responses in entries [1] to [4].

1. What does the teacher do after Margie gives an abrupt "No"?
2. Check Ryan's response in entry [12]. Which question is he answering?

*See Chapter 9, page 103.

3. If you had been the teacher and wished to stay with the first question longer, what second question would you have asked?
4. Which three children gave the explanation for their thinking without being asked?
5. It seems children of this age usually give their explanation with a "because" clause. Note how Ryan frames his explanation of his thinking.
6. How do you think Ryan felt in entry [16] as he gave his last response to the teacher?

The use of this sequence is not meant to imply that all the children in this class could think as independently as Ryan nor at his level, but rather that all children should be invited and have the opportunity to lift the level of their thinking. During the first part of the discussion where the children spoke from memory (giving data) as the teacher charted, twenty-four different children gave one-hundred-nineteen responses. After the teacher asked them to make predictions as to "what if——?", four entered the discussion. This is about what one would expect when children are not accustomed to such questions.

DISCUSSION SEQUENCE

Poor Readers Learn to Consider What Others Think

Class Description

This third grade was located in a farming area of California. Many of the children were migrant. The class was described as "slow". The taping took place in the spring of the year.

Focus of Discussion

The class had completed its study of desert nomads and had been discussing the changes that might take place if suddenly the desert could have all the water it needed. Many "chains of change" had been developed around: (1) ways of earning a living; (2) growth of towns; (3) education, etc.

At this point the teacher injected the idea of how people feel about change. The following sequence took place:

[1] **Teacher:** With all these changes in the desert, what would happen to the old ways of life?

Deborah: They would be forgotten and they wouldn't use them any more.

Ronald: They probably would use them, because their ancestors—just like in Hong Kong. They don't quit doing what their ancestors done.

Donna: Well, there would be quite a lot of changes.

[5] Teacher: What kind of changes?

Donna: Well, their jobs.

Teacher: What do you think the old nomads, the old people, would think of this new way of life?

Freddie: Well, they wouldn't like it too much, because they would probably want to stick to the way that their ancestors did it.

Brenda: It would probably be strange to them.

[10] Teacher: Strange in what way?

Deborah: They would feel sort of funny—like they were just being born and all that.

Duke: I don't think the old people would like it too much, because they would think their way was better.

Teacher: Why?

Duke: Because they was taught it, and they want their sons to do the same thing. Anyway, they would grouch.

[15] Deborah: In a couple of years they would start changing and year by year, pretty soon, they would be modern.

Teacher: What do you think the children would think about this?

Mark: They would probably think that they had a new world.

Deborah: They wouldn't think it was so important. But their parents would think it was more important, because they have been that way more years than the children have.

POINTS FOR THOUGHT

*Deborah Modifies Her Thinking***

After you have read the discussion sequence, reread Deborah's three responses in entries [2], [15], and [18].

**See Chapter 9, page 103.

1. What has happened to her thinking in this short sequence?
2. How do you account for this change?
3. Which speakers (teacher or children) do you think might have influenced Deborah?
4. How many children volunteer their reason for their prediction?
5. Note that the only "why" question [13] the teacher asked was of a child who had just given his reason for a statement, but it brought forth a good piece of thinking. Many times the second "why" is answered with a shrug of the shoulders.
6. Reread Ronald's response in entry [3]. Earlier in the year, the class had studied a unit on changes taking place in the community of boat people in Hong Kong. It is unusual for an eight year old to apply a generalization spontaneously to explain a new situation.

CHAPTER 7

Roles to Be Assumed by Teacher/Child

"READING THE FEEDBACK" AND ASSUMING THE APPROPRIATE ROLE

NO set of questions alone will meet the needs of every discussion. As the teacher "reads the feedback" from the students, he/she, on his/her feet, must provide supporting questions and assume one of a variety of roles. "Reading the feedback" requires knowledge of both children and subject matter, alertness to possible new insights or misconceptions, and sensitivity to the length of time one can "hang in" with one child. Such skills make the teacher indispensable in classroom discussions.

Role of Clarifier

Students rarely ask for clarification. Often the teacher who asks, "Could you tell us a little more?" sets an example that encourages the students to ask more often, "What do you mean by that?"

The excerpt below shows a teacher who asked the critical question that elicited an important idea from a child. The discussion was taped in a second-grade classroom.

Child: It says in this book that the moon is 250,000 miles from the earth but on the record it is 240,000 miles.

Teacher: Do you have any idea why these two different figures might have been given?

Child: Maybe the book was written after the record was made.

Teacher: What difference would that make?

Child: Well, people study all the time and the longer people study, the more you learn about things.

While not an explanation for the difference between the two figures the response of the child to the crucial question, "What difference would that make?" revealed his thinking and contributed a new idea to the class—the accumulation of knowledge.

Role of the Synthesizer

When a student or several students give a number of ideas in response to a question, the teacher might well ask, "Can you put that into fewer words?" Some students seem to develop into synthesizers at a very early age. An example is given below of a fourth grader of whom the teacher said, "She always ties a ribbon around what has been said and hands it to me."

The class had been talking about some factors that help to determine the pricing of products (i.e., good fish, big pieces of gold, straight cotton). The teacher asked, "Can somebody tell me what kinds of things help to decide the price of the thing that is being sold."

John: If you went to the store and you'd pay . . . (I don't know how much you'd pay) . . . and when you came home and it wasn't a very good fish, well, it wouldn't be fair.

Teacher: It wouldn't be fair. That's one idea.

Jean: But how big it is, is important. You have a little tiny piece of gold that's worth five dollars, and then you have a great big piece and do you think that's going to cost only five dollars?

Teacher: You're thinking of size, aren't you Jean? Ruby.

Ruby: Well, cotton—like it will have to be straight—some of it might not be straight and it's not as good as the other.

Teacher: Does someone want to put those things into a few words for us? Esther?

Esther: Well, the better the quality, the better the thing you have is, the higher the price.

Role of Supporter

Another role, usually assumed by the teacher, is that of offering support to a student whose contribution has been rejected by other students. If the teacher can put the problem in a larger context by saying "This is something all of us need to work on," it helps all the students, especially the one being challenged.

A student who gives incorrect information is usually in need of support. The teacher needs to help him correct his own error and help him re-enter the discussion as soon as possible. One goal of a productive discussion is to help students learn to become increasingly aware of what other students say and to build on their contributions. An effective way to move the student toward that goal is to invite children to add to what others have said, to have another point of view, and to remain alert to what others are saying by referring to what (so-and-so) said by name.

As they mature, students must become less dependent on adults as the final authorities and dispensers of support. This is why a teacher must try to make his students feel comfortable about disagreeing in a socially acceptable manner with him and other students. When a student says, "Isn't that right, Mr. Smith?", Mr. Smith must decide whether the student needs support, or whether this is the time to help him/her become increasingly autonomous by encouraging the student to state his/her own views and reasons.

DISCUSSION SEQUENCE

Why We Make Choices in a Given Situation[9]

Class Description

This discussion involved a group of fourth-grade children who as second graders had been considered a problem class. In the third grade with Ms. Kelley they had improved so much in both academic skills and behavior that the teacher was asked to move to the fourth grade with the class. This taping was made in the spring of the class' second year with Ms. Kelley.

Materials

The students had written on cards the name or names of students they would like to work with on a committee. Ms. Kelley then interviewed each student on his/her basis for each choice. She referred to the cards and interviews but gave no information children had given her. Ms. Kelley always kept a tape recorder in her room ready for spontaneous discussions.

[9]From materials developed by Intergroup Education Project sponsored by American Council on Education, Washington, D.C., 1948.

Focus

Ms. Kelley focused the discussion on why people are chosen on a somewhat different basis for different jobs, yet certain characteristics are present in all choices.

[1] Ms. Kelley: From the cards you have handed in and the reasons you have given me when I have interviewed you about the people you have chosen for committee work or group work, it seems to me some of you are beginning to have rather definite ideas in mind when you make your choices. I thought it maybe might help us all to make better choices and also to be better group workers if we could talk together this morning about some of the reasons we choose people with whom we want to work. If you are appointed chairman of a group, what are the things you would consider in choosing people to work with you?

Lawrence: First, I would want to know what kind of a committee it was. Some people would be good at one thing but not so hot doing something else.

Regina: That's a good idea! I'd love to have Wayne on my committee if I was illustrating a book, but he wouldn't be much good if we were writing music for a song.

Wayne: I guess I wouldn't. (All laughed because Wayne couldn't carry a tune at all.) And you won't be so hot on the committee to build booths.

[5] Regina: I'd be all right if you had plenty Merthiolate handy. (This was all friendly banter, for Regina couldn't drive a nail without banging her finger.)

Ellen: They really are right. You gotta know what the committee is for and pick somebody who can do that thing. Else you won't get far.

Dick: That's sure important, but I'd think about the way people act too. A person might be an awful good drawer, but if he acted silly and wasted time foolin' around, he wouldn't be no good on our art committee.

Ellen: Yeah, that's right too, Dick! And people who all the time say crazy things won't help much neither.

Joanne: I would want people on my committee who had good ideas too. But I'd want them to not talk all the time but give somebody else a chance to tell their ideas.

[10] Ronnie: I agree with Joanne. If you have good ideas you oughta share 'em 'cause can't everybody have good ideas about everything. But you oughta listen some too. You're not the only person who has good ideas and sometimes something somebody says gives you better ideas.

Joanne: That's what I mean. We can help by listening sometimes, too.

Donna: Especially to directions. You remember all the trouble David got into last year 'cause he didn't listen to Ms. Kelley when she explained how to cut the paper to cover the screen. Then, I did wonder why you didn't help him, Ms. Kelley, but now I know it was because he wouldn't listen when you told him and you wanted to show him that sometimes it was important to listen. Wasn't that it?

Ms. Kelley: Yes, Donna, but not only so David would realize that. I don't suppose you can remember that far back, but I do. At that time none of you listened too well to direction and I think it helped you all to realize the importance of listening to directions.

Patty B.: Was that 'bout the time we started listening better?

[15] Ms. Kelley: I think so.

Patty O.: Another important thing if we are choosing a committee is whether people can be depended on or not. I mean whether they do what they say they will.

Louis: That's right, if we say we'll do something we ought to. (Here Louis really threw himself open to trouble!)

Jack: You're right!

Mike: You sure ought, Louie!

[20] Margaret: When did you decide that, Louis?

Dick: Well, do you really say so! (The above four remarks were simultaneous but I recorded them all because other students really were disappointed with Louis' failure to follow through on promises.)

Louis: Well, ain't I done better lately. Ain't I brought everything I said I would for the bazaar. I do think that's important! And don't I keep my mouth shut now less I do what I say?

Ms. Kelley: You — (she stopped because Donald started at the same time).

Donald: Yes, he has. He brought four orange crates — that's one more than he said he would — and that big box.

[25] Lawrence: Yes, and he's brought his wagon and helped carry the paper down twice. I think we ought to forget what he did before, if he keeps on doing what he says now.

Louis: I think so too!

Ms. Kelley: So do I. Haven't you all changed and grown in your way of doing things? And that is the important thing. I'm sure you all want us to think of you as you are now, not as you were last year or last fall or even last month. Louis has tried very hard and is now often quite dependable.

Dick: You're right Ms. Kelley. I'm sorry. It is important and I guess we all need to remember that.

Mike: I'd think about whether people are lazy or not before I picked 'em. If everybody don't do their part then somebody else has to work awful hard and that's not fair cause it could keep you from finishing on time.

[30] Shirley: Another thing I think is important is whether they are considerate of other people.

Ms. Kelley: That is a rather indefinite statement, Shirley. Could you explain more clearly what you mean?

Shirley: Well if they interrupt when people are talking that makes you not get so much done. And if they don't share the tools that's not helping either.

Abreena: I don't think they help either when they make fun of people's ideas. Then people are afraid to tell their ideas.

Wayne: Another thing that's not being considerate is making fun when people have done the best they can. That makes them feel bad and they don't do anything the next time.

[35] Adam: Something else I'd think about is whether they could get along with the other people I chose. If you have somebody in a group who can't get along with somebody else, they can cause lots of trouble. There's a boy over to Kingswood that can't get along with people and he always causes trouble.

Ellen: I wouldn't want nobody on my committee who wouldn't cooperate and I think you gotta do all those things to cooperate.

Ms. Kelley: I think you are right, Ellen. I wonder if we could quickly summarize the things we have been talking about and have Regina put them on the board.

Mike: Could we call it "What a Good Committee Member Does?"

Ms. Kelley: If you would like.

What follows is Regina's listing of what a good committee member does as the class dictated it.

(*1*) They got to know something about the thing the committee is supposed to do.

(*2*) They got to know how to keep their mind on what they are doing and not act silly.

(*3*) They got to listen to directions and follow them sometimes.

(*4*) They got to do what they are supposed to and say they will so you can depend on them.

(*5*) They are willing to do their part.

(*6*) They are considerate of other people's feelings.

(*7*) They can get along with people.

(*8*) They cooperate.

[40] Ms. Kelley: I think this is a very good set of standards for choosing people to work with. As I look at them though, I wonder if you would use the same set if you were choosing people for a social situation, a party, or movie, or trip with you.

Patty O.: Oh no! Leastways, I wouldn't. The most important thing would be whether I liked them or not. I wouldn't ask anybody to a party that I didn't like.

Patty B.: Neither would I, but I'd think about the way they behave too. I wouldn't want somebody that yelled and jumped on the furniture and acted about six years old.

Barbara: No, neither would I. And I'd not ask them again if they weren't good sports neither. I had a party last year and one of the kids wouldn't play nothing but hopscotch and just sat and looked mean when all the rest played hide-and-seek.

Regina: Neither would I, Barbie, and another thing I'd think about is whether they play fair or not. That's important too.

[45] Jack: Yes, and I'd think did they like the same things as me.

Patty O.: Something else makes a difference in who you ask to do things with you, is who your mother says you can. (Several: "Yeah, that's so; that's right Pat; etc.")

Ms. Kelley: How many of you have had your mother refuse to allow you to invite someone you wanted to a social function? (Several hands went up.) Why?

Patty B. I wanted to ask a girl that my mother said was too old. She was twelve and I was eight.

Joanne: I did the same thing. I think now that she wouldn't have wanted to come anyway. She was too old.

[50] Patty B.: I guess my mother was right.

Margaret: Well, my mother might have been right but I don't know her well enough. Well, she didn't but I did and she ought to trust me.

Donna: Margaret, that happens all the time. My mother don't like me to invite people she don't know either but how else can she know them.

Mike: Mine too! It's "Who is this so and so?" all the time.

Ms. Kelley: Could that be another problem of growing up?

[55] Mike: Yeah, I guess so. Some parts of growing up are fine but others are kinda tough!!! (Several sighed and agreed.)

Ms. Kelley: Well, it seems to me that most of you and your parents are working out your problems of growing up rather satisfactorily. I think we just about have time now to summarize the reasons we would use in choosing people for social situations and compare them with our first list. Margaret, would you write those for us.

What follows is a list of reasons for choosing persons to be part of social situations.

(*1*) Because I like them and they like me.

(*2*) They know how to behave.

(*3*) They are good sports.

(*4*) They play fair.

(*5*) They like the same things I do.

(*6*) Your mother likes them too.

Joanne: Ms. Kelley, I think we ought to add another one to that list. I'd think about how they treat other people.

Regina: That's how they behave.

Dick: No, it's not just the same.

[60] Don: I don't think so either. I think it ought to be added.

Ms. Kelley: How many want it added? (All did, so it was.)

Ms. Kelley: Do you see any similar ideas on these lists?

Lawrence: Yes, #3 on list #2, and #2 on list #1.

Patty O.: I think #4 on list #2, and #5 on list #1.

[65] Wayne: Aren't #6 and #7 on list #1 and #7 and #2 about the same?

Ms. Kelley: Then would you say there are some things we consider whenever we choose other people to be with?

Regina: Yes, how they behave, how they treat other people, and whether they cooperate or not.

Ms. Kelley: I think so. And don't you think we should remember that if that is what we look for in others, they also look for that in us?

POINTS FOR THOUGHT

Matching Roles and Questions/Responses*

1. Directions: After you have read the total discussion sequence, reread the question or response identified by the number in brackets, e.g., [5]. The number refers to the total response, not the line alone. Check the list of roles given and decide what role you think the speaker is assuming. Enter the <u>role</u> on the space provided next to the name, and, when appropriate, explain what is happening.

Roles

To set focus	To elicit interference,
To initiate new ideas	generalization, or
To extend an old idea	summary
To refocus	To recap
To clarify	To synthesize
To support	To change focus

Teacher/Child Response Number

Ms. K. [1] _____

Lawrence [2] _____

Regina [3] _____

Ellen [6] _____

Dick [7] _____

Joanne [9] _____

Ronnie [10] _____

*See Chapter 9, page 105.

Ms. K. [13] _____

Patty O. [16] _____

Louis [17] to Ms. K. [23]. What is happening here? _____

_____

Donald [24] _____

Lawrence [25] _____

Louis [26] _____

Ms. K. [27] _____

Mike [29] _____

Ms. K. [31] _____

Ellen [36] _____

Ms. K. [40] _____

Ms. K. [56] _____

2. Which child generalized more than once? _____
3. How often did Ms. Kelley refocus the discussion? _____
4. How often did students refocus? _____
5. Check responses [57] to [62]. How did Ms. Kelley handle the difference in point of view? When would that method be inappropriate? _____
_____
_____

6. What can you say about the atmosphere in Ms. Kelley's classroom? _____
_____
_____

Strategies for Interpersonal Problem Solving/ Analysis of Values/Exploring Feelings

INTERPERSONAL PROBLEM SOLVING

FOR six years prior to coming to San Francisco State University, Dr. Taba was director of the project on Intergroup Education in Cooperating Schools of the American Council on Education and under the auspices of the Center for Intergroup Education at the University of Chicago. Studies undertaken by Dr. Taba and her staff were designed to describe ideas, tools, and procedures that might be used by teachers to develop an integrated program on problems of human relations.

The staff of the Taba Curriculum Development Project recognized that these terms have a variety of meanings and implications and that comparatively little was known about the outcome of in-school procedures in this area. Nevertheless, a considerable body of theory and some research suggest that it should be possible to devise teaching strategies to help attain objectives in this domain.

The strategies presented are designed to provide students with practice in (1) considering various approaches to solving disputes among persons and groups; (2) analyzing values held by people, including themselves; and (3) exploring feelings—their own and others'.

Strategy for Interpersonal Problem Solving

Students are presented with a problem involving interpersonal conflict. Questioning proceeds according to the strategy presented in Table 8.1.[10]

[10]Adapted from *Reading Ladders for Human Relations* by Margaret Heaton and Helen Lewis. American Council on Education, Washington, D.C.

TABLE 8.1.

Teacher	Students	Teacher Follow-Through
What happened? or What did . . . do?	Describes events.	Sees that all events are given or, if not possible, a clear statement of differences in perception of what occurred.
What do you think a (protagonist) should do? Why?	Gives response.	Accepts response; seeks clarification where necessary.
How do you think (others) would react if he/she did that? Why?	Makes inference and explains.	Accepts response; seeks clarification if necessary.
Has anything like that ever happened to you?	Relates similar event in his own life.	Provides support, if necessary.
What did you do?	Relates recalled behavior.	Seeks clarification, if necessary.
As you think back now, do you think that was a good or a bad thing to do?	Judges past action.	Encourages student to judge his/her own past actions. Teacher may need to prevent others from entering the discussion at this point.
Why do you think so?	States reasons.	Accepts reasons; if necessary, asks additional questions to make clear the criteria or values the student is using in judging his actions.
Is their anything you could have done differently?	Offers alternative behavior.	Accepts; asks additional questions to point up inconsistencies where they occur, i.e., "How does that agree with the reasons you gave earlier?

DISCUSSION SEQUENCE

Eva, the New Girl from Puerto Rico

Class Description

The taping of the dialogue below was done with a class of thirty-four third graders. It was a group with a wide range of academic skills and emotional stability. At the time of the taping, Eva had been in the school for three weeks. She was the only black child in the school. This was a community serving a farming area which was fast changing into a commuting community. In the fall, this class didn't seem able to identify a problem—just accuse and vent anger; this discussion took place in the spring.

Materials

A tape recorder. The teacher kept a tape recorder available to catch any spur-of-the-moment event that might give insight into the problems of these children.

Focus

The teacher had no time to prepare a particular sequence of questions but her experience in keeping the children focusing on one problem is reflected in her questioning here. The children identified two problems, but the teacher pursues one.

As the children entered the classroom after lunch, Harry told Ms. S. about the name-calling. She arranged with the librarian to invite Eva to help her shelve books. Eva was not in the room during the discussion.

[1] Teacher: Harry has a problem he'd like to bring up before this class to discuss and think about.

Harry: Today I was walking with Eva to school and she said, "One reason I don't like Burnside—because I don't have no friends." And I asked her why, and she said that—just like today—"They were calling me nigger."

Teacher: Harry, that's very startling news. Does anyone have anything else to say? Lex?

Lex: Well, I don't like other people calling people names like that.

Maybe they have different color skin but I agree with Harry, I don't like anybody or anybody of that sort, or anything of that sort going around in this school, because, well, we try to make it a good school.

[5] Girl: Well one day—today, when I tried to tell Eva to play in a good game, well, she told me people were calling her <u>names</u> like that.

Donald: Ms. S., just a few days ago when I was playing tether ball, this kid, he-they-Eva really won the game, but he's a little pimpered [*sic*] kid and he started to call her nig-Negro and I didn't care too much for that at all.

Teacher: Did you do anything about it, Donald?

Donald: Well, there was nothing I could do much, but John Evans knows what to say really.

John E.: Ms. S., it's Jerry Smith and Linda. They were playing tether ball and they were getting along fine with (pause) and then Eva won, and I came over and everybody, and she comes up and says, "John, they're calling me nigger." And he started to hit me so I hit back, and he told his teacher. And I went in to the teacher and said, "Teacher, I don't want any of your boys calling our new girl a Negro," and she said, "That's right" and I figure Eva has a lot—I figure these boys right here—they want more friends, they want more friends really, Jerry Smith and Linda want more friends but they just don't know how to get them. How would you feel—I know how I would feel if I was new here and I was playing a good game and somebody called me a Negro. How would you feel? I wouldn't feel very good, I'd feel like nobody wanted me, Ms. S.

[10] Teacher: Does anyone else have anything to say? Karl?

Karl: Well I was with John, and we—I was in line, I was first one in line, and Eva really won him—but—his real name is Jeff Carson and the yard teacher said that when he doesn't go out when he's lost for us to go on in. So I went on in and he started calling her names and Negro and stuff. Then John came along and we tried to stop him. Then we went in and told his teacher and she said she would talk to him.

Teacher: Now, wait. We're getting outside of our class a little bit. Harry, would you say that Eva felt she had no friends? Is that what she said? All right. Who are her classmates? I see all of your hands up. Let's talk to that point and leave the children in the other room out for just a moment.

I know Eva is new, I know that, and we've talked about the fact that she has a different nationality, her hair is somewhat different and her skin is a different color, but how do you feel about those things? I'm interested in what you think and feel and how Eva thinks and feels. Betsy?

Betsy: I think that—I don't care what color her skin is, I think that she's fun to play with, she's like the other kids. She's no different from the other kids.

Teacher: Clara?

[15] Clara: Well, remember how you said she didn't have the same color hair or skin? Well, she does have the same blood that we have and I think it's a shame for kids to be calling her "nigger."

Teacher: Anybody else. Fred?

Fred: Well, anyway, we all have the same insides. The same feelings about each other.

Teacher: Fred, you've come upon something so important. John?

John: Well I think she's pretty nice. When we had these cards to make about who misbehaved when you were out of the room, she didn't put anything on it about anybody.

[20] Teacher: Anybody else? Susan?

Susan: Well, I think even if she does have different color skin and hair, it doesn't make a difference, she's no different, you could still play with her, she's nice too, and I think she's a nice girl to play with.

Teacher: I think you children have a real wonderful feeling about Eva, but Eva still feels that she hasn't any friends. Is she right in feeling that way? Laurie?

Laurie: Well, whenever we'd see her on the playground or something like that, we wouldn't tell her that she is a different color than us or anything, we'd go over and ask her if she'd like to come and play, and then she'd feel like she has more friends.

Teacher: That's a solution. Has that happened? Susan?

[25] Susan: Well, I don't think so—but I think it's not true because she has lots of friends.

Teacher: Does she? Can anybody remember the very first day Eva came into school, about three weeks ago? Who was appointed to be her special friend that day? Can you remember, Betsy?

Betsy: Well, her special friend was, I think, Margie Kolb.

Teacher: Margie, can you tell us what you did to make Eva feel at home in our school?

Margie: Played Four Squares.

[30] Teacher: Do anything else? (pause) Did anyone else do anything to make Eva feel at home in our school? Clara, what did you do?

Clara: Well, when it was eleven o'clock recess, I asked Eva whether she wanted to play tether ball and she said, "Yes," and I showed her how to play tether ball.

Teacher: Marian? Susan?

Susan: Well, one time Eva was sitting alone and I came up and asked her if she wanted to play with me, so we played Follow the Leader.

Teacher: Marian? . . . (pause). Marian, do you have anything to say? Have you tried to make Eva a part of the class?

[35] Marian: No.

Teacher: Have you tried to make Eva a part of the class, Jack?

Jack: Yes.

Teacher: Have you tried to make Eva a part of the class, Harry?

Harry: Yes.

Teacher: In what way, Harry?

[40] Harry: Well, I asked her if she wanted to play Four Squares when she was new.

Teacher: When she was new. Well, that was three weeks ago. What about this week?

Harry: Well, I haven't seen her around much.

Teacher: John?

John: Lex and me were walking around the playground, and we had nothing to do, and she was walking around, and we got into a game of Four Squares, the three of us, and we told her how to play and made sure she had a fair chance and everything. I think we did quite good.

[45] Teacher: Let me see a raise of hands of how many people in the class think that sometimes, when we know a person is really new, we make more of an effort to make friends with them. And then after the newness is worn off, then we kind of forget. Forget. Is that a natural thing to do? How many think we should take those things for granted? Lex?

Lex: Well, I don't think it's actually right, because you have lots of friends and-but-when you make new friends, well, that means you should play with your old friends and get the new friends to play with them too. And to go on and get too many friends. Well, gee, I—I think it's just downright ri-dic-u-lous (laughter) to forget any friends.

Teacher: To forget any.

Lex: Yeah. Well, Ms. S., when we play Four Square, she always asks us if it's a boy's game. I guess some of the boys don't let her play Four Squares.

Teacher: Well, you could probably consider this, too: Eva's been in another school and perhaps in the other school, they separated the children and she's not used to playing with us in a group as we do in our school, all the games being open. Eric, have you something to say?

[50] Eric: Well, Eva's a nice girl and she come from another country and she's a pretty nice girl.

Teacher: Yes, Eric, I think we've all come to the conclusion that she is a nice girl, but let's go back to this one fact — she hasn't any special friends. What can we do about it; is there anything we can do about it? You know, I don't pick your friends, do I? What could we really do about it? Jimmy?

Jimmy: Well, they can make friends.

Teacher: Well, how could we? Let's just be very — let's just pick some ways.

Jimmy: Well, we can go up to her and ask her if she can play Four Squares or tether ball or anything like that.

[55] Teacher: Betsy?

Betsy: Well, I think if we all go and ask her at once, I think she'll feel kind of funny inside, so I think we should just maybe choose about one or two.

Teacher: I think, Betsy, you're being very sensible. Karen?

Karen: Well, I don't think Eva had a turn to play on the animals that they put in our school so if one of us sees her and she has nobody to play with, they could ask her if she would like to go and play on the new things they have put up.

Teacher: Ed.

[60] Ed: Eva loves to play tether ball and I think some of us kids who know how to play tether ball could go over and play with her in the same game that she is playing in and I think she would appreciate that — and find out that we are trying to help her get more friends.

Teacher: Let's go back now. I know by listening to you and seeing what a real concern you have, what are we going to do about people who are not understanding of this difference she has in her physical appearance? We know that we're not different, I can tell that from the way you're talking, but what about the people who don't have that understanding? Can we do anything about that as a class?

Class: Yes!

Teacher: Harry, you brought up the problem. Do you think we can do anything about these other people on the grounds who are not as thoughtful as they should be, and who feel that there is a real difference because a person's hair and their skin is a different color? Can we do anything about it?

Harry: Yes, I mean we can just have the person who said it go up and say, "I'm sorry," and stuff. I think that helps a little bit.

[65] Teacher: How are you going to do that though? Are you going to do that in front of Eva?

Harry: No.

Teacher: How would you do that, Harry? Would you fight about it?

Harry: No, we wouldn't, because that would be mean too.

Teacher: All right, how would you take care of this boy that was out on the grounds and called her "nigger"? How would you take care of that?

[70] Harry: I wouldn't like it, I don't think they should be at our school.

Teacher: Oh, but they're here, and their folks live here and they are taxpayers.

Harry: Yes, but how—how would you like to be called a "nigger"? I wouldn't.

Teacher: Well, how are we going to take care of the problem? Harry, can we solve it in any way? How would you solve it—someone who hasn't spoken up—Laurie?

Laurie: Well, I would solve it by taking the person up to her to tell her they're sorry or giving them a punishment.

[75] Teacher: How would you, a little girl, punish a big boy?

Laurie: Have the yard teacher get after them.

Teacher: You mean, you might go to the yard teacher and tell the yard teacher? That's one way. Another way? Clara.

Clara: Well, I think that some of these kids could, you know, get up a group and ask her if she wants to play something, a new game.

Teacher: Clara, we're talking how we can get those children from another room to feel about Eva the way you do. Lex?

[80] Lex: Well, well, well—I think we ought to get friendly with some of these kids, you know, and sort of play and then say, "Well, now, like Eva, well, she's my friend," and I'd say, "I want you to meet my friend, Eva." And then, you know, make it sort of, well, like you said, a right out of a wrong.

Teacher: Make a right out of a wrong? What about these boys and their understanding? Or should I say, a misunderstanding, isn't it?

Class: Yes.

Teacher: How can you erase that misunderstanding? First of all, I think it's wonderful that you want to make real friends, and introduce her (Eva) as your friend but how can you make a right out of a wrong and erase this misunderstanding? Donald?

Donald: Well, you have said this before, I don't know how many times, and it's always worked out; forgive and forget. You've always said that and it's always worked out.

[85] Teacher: Yes, but this boy who's been doing this, maybe more than once, is that right, Harry?

Harry: Yes.

Teacher: What are we going to do about him, how can we clear this up?

Harry: Ms. S., I think if that boy would come up, even, say, "Let's have a good game of Four Squares, OK?" And then he goes over there and he plays with her.

Teacher: But don't you think that boy needs some education?

[90] Class: Yes.

Teacher: Bill, how do you think that boy could learn this?

Bill: Well . . . I don't know. By, I guess, by someone goin' up to him, and saying, "How would you like to feel, and all, like Eva does now?"

Teacher: Anybody else have a solution? Ted?

Ted: Well, I think if he just listened to this tape and had his teacher tell him that he ought to like Eva, the nice things about her and have him listen to this tape. I think that would help doing it.

[95] Teacher: How many think that would be one way we could broach this problem? Having him know how other children feel about her? Well, that's a solution. Any other solutions? Laurie? (no answers)

Teacher: Any other solutions? Well, Harry, have we taken care of this problem? We haven't finished the problem, have we? Let's summarize real quickly:

- This class does not have that feeling against children of another color.
- Maybe we have forgotten that she still needs friends. And we're going to do something about that, not all at once, are we, as Betsy said.
- We're going to try to get these boys who have these misunderstandings cleared up, straighten them out.

And in doing that, we're going to be as friendly as we can. Is that right? All right. Well, I think that's fine. Let's watch and see how things go and let's all bend and make a special effort to be friends with everybody. All right. Fine.

POINTS FOR THOUGHT

Pursuing a Problem, Sensitivity to the Feelings of Others, and Offering Solutions*

1. Reread the complete script of Eva, the New Girl from Puerto Rico.
2. Who states the problem? _____
3. Actually two problems are given. What are they?
   a. _____
   b. _____
4. Which problem does the teacher focus on? _____
   _____
5. Why do you suppose she chose that one? _____
   _____

6. The question and responses from entries [1] through [50] deal largely with identifying the problem and the class' attitude about the situation. In entry [51] the teacher changes the focus. What does she ask the children to consider? _____
   _____

   Would you have asked a different question at that point? ____
   If yes, what would you have asked? _____
   _____

*See Chapter 9, page 105.

7. Assume you have read a story to the class about Betty, a sixth-grader, who is so bossy that finally the rest of the class leaves her out of all the activities.

8. Rearrange (by numbering them) the following questions into a logical sequence appropriate for sensitizing experiences:

_____ Has anything like this ever happened to you?

_____ How do you think Betty felt about this?

_____ What happened in the story?

_____ How do you think Betty's classmates felt when they left her out?

_____ How did you feel?

_____ How might the situation have been different?

9. Select a film, filmstrip or book that provides an episode for a discussion of feelings, attitudes, or conflict. Plan a question sequence that you would use in a classroom.

Summary of the episode:

Question sequence:

ANALYSIS OF VALUES

Students are asked to recall certain behaviors and are asked to make inferences about what values are involved, and how they differ from the values of others involved in analogous situations. Strategies of questioning to elicit inferences are found in Table 8.2.[11]

ANALYZING ANOTHER'S VALUES AND ONE'S OWN VALUES IN COMPARABLE SITUATIONS

In the strategy, Analyzing Values, the teacher asks the child to examine his or her own values in comparable situations. The responses the child gives in considering how he/she would act do not guarantee what his/her behavior would be; but it is hoped he/she will grow in awareness of the relationship between what is claimed to be believed and actions and speech.

Assume a class of fifth graders has studied the period of the Revolutionary War. They have seen the film *John Yankee: John Adams and the Boston Massacre,* which tells of John Adams' defense of an accused British soldier.

[11]Wallen et al. 1969. *Final Report,* p. 29.

TABLE 8.2.

Teacher	Students	Teacher Follow-Through
What did they do . . . (e.g., to take care of their tools)?	Describes behavior.	Sees that description is complete and accurate.
What do you think were their reasons for doing/saying what they did?	States inferences.	Accepts; seeks clarification, if necessary.
What do these reasons tell you about what is important to them?	States inferences.	Restates or asks additional questions to insure focus on values.
If you . . . (teacher specifies similar situations directly related to student, e.g., "if you accidentally tore a page in someone's book,") what would you do? Why?	States behavior.	Accepts; may seek clarification.
What does this show about what <u>you</u> think is important?	States inferences about his own values.	Accepts; seeks clarification, if necessary.
What differences do you see in what all these people think is important?	Makes comparisons.	Insures that all values identified are compared.

Following the viewing of the film the teacher asked:

(*1*) What happened in the film?

(*2*) What reason did John Adams give for defending the British soldier?

(*3*) What do these reasons tell you about what John Adams thought was important?

Distribute written copies of the situation below and let each student respond to it:

Suppose you were proud of the valuable collection of baseball cards your grandfather had given you. Your mother said they were too valuable to take to school but she finally let you. There was a new boy named Duke in your class. You and your friends didn't like him. Duke came up to look when your friends were passing the cards around out on the playground. Several boys told him to go away. When the bell rang you couldn't find out who had the cards. As soon as you reached the classroom, you told the teacher your baseball cards were missing. The teacher asked all to raise their desktops. He went to each desk and found the cards in Duke's desk. What do you think should be done and why?

___The cards were valuable so the police should be called.

___Duke should be expelled from school.

___He should be allowed to tell his side of the story.

___Duke should be allowed to go free with no questions.

___(Some other idea for handling the problem)

Let the students share their recommendations and why they made them. Encourage them to think of arguments Duke might have made. (Had Duke left the group when they told him to go? Had someone who didn't like him put the cards in his desk? Had someone meant to put them in the owner's desk but got them in the wrong desk?) What does your choice of action tell you about what you think is important? Select responses from several who have indicated they thought "a trial" or "defense" should always be allowed and ask:

What "right" are these people saying all should have?

GENERALIZING ABOUT ANOTHER'S VALUES AND RELATING THEM TO ONE'S OWN VALUES

Inferring or generalizing about the values of others (persons or countries) is often appropriate as the class discusses the contributions or exploits of historical figures. Inferences or generalizations about values can be handled by using the strategy, Developing Generalizations, as shown in the following.

Assume a class of fourth graders has studied the waves of different people who came to what is now the state of California (Indians, Spaniards, Americans from the East, '49ers). Contrast the experiences of the people of California with those of a sampling of people who came to the province of Nova Scotia (Micmacs, Acadians, English, Blacks from America, and Scots). The teacher has planned to have the students consider the values held by Boston King, the leader of a group of Blacks most of whom were or had been slaves. The raw data for the discussion was charted on the chalkboard. The teacher planned the following questions for the discussion:

(*1*) When the American colonists were fighting the British, what did many of the slaves do?

(2) If slaves were caught running away, what might happen to them?

(3) Who was the leader of some of the slaves?

(4) What plan did Boston King work out with the British?

(5) What does this action of King and the slaves tell you they thought was important?

(6) Have you ever felt trapped (been in a situation you wanted to get out of)? What did you do? What does this show about what's important to you?

(7) Have you known of other people who thought freedom was important? What did they do about it?

(8) What does this tell you about how people generally act if they really think something is important?

EXPLORING FEELINGS

Students are presented with a situation involving emotional reactions on the part of one or more persons. The teaching strategy consists of asking the following questions, usually in the order presented in Table 8.3.[12]

CASE HISTORY

Walk the World's Rim

Class Description

The sixth-grade class involved in the following discussion was in a school referred to variously as target area, ghetto, or economically disadvantaged. The students were predominantly African-American, from an extremely low socioeconomic background, and in general had considerably below-average academic skills.

When the schedule for the first taping was being planned, the consultant asked the teacher at what level most of the students read. She replied, "It's hard to know. Most of them scored around the second-grade level on standardized reading tests. However, they approach every test expecting to fail. These children have never known success in the classroom. Practically every question I ask is answered by a shrug of the shoulders or monosyllabic response."

[12]Wallen et al. 1969. *Final Report*, p. 27.

TABLE 8.3.

Teacher	Students	Teacher Follow-Through
What happened?	Restates facts.	Sees that all facts are given and agreed upon. If students make inferences, asks that they be postponed.
How do you think . . . felt?	Makes inferences as to feelings.	Accepts inferences.
Why do you think he/she would feel that way?	Explains.	Seeks clarification if necessary.
Who has a different opinion about how he/she feels?	Makes alternative inferences and explanations.	Seeks variety, if necessary. Asks for reasons, if necessary.
How did . . . (other persons in the situation) feel?	States inferences about the feelings of additional persons.	Seeks clarification, if necessary; encourages students to consider how other people in the situation felt.
Have you ever had something like this happen to you?	Describes similar events in his/her own life.	Insures description of event.
How did you feel?	Describes his feelings; may re-experience emotions.	Seeks clarification, if necessary. Provides support, if necessary.
Why do you think you felt that way?	Offers explanation; attempts to relate his feelings to events he has recalled.	Asks additional questions, if necessary, to get beyond stereotyped or superficial explanations.

The first videotaping was a disaster; the classroom was so noisy the audio was a jumble of sound, the pupils wandered aimlessly, and there was a considerable incidence of verbal hostility between students. By spring, however, as will be seen from the dialogue below, the students not only were able to respond at high levels of proficiency for their age, but also gave evidence of considerable interest in the activity itself.

Materials

During several social studies periods preceding the taping of this discussion the teacher had been reading the book *Walk the World's Rim* by B. Baker, a story based on historical figures and incidents that took place at the time of the Spanish conquest of Mexico. At the taping the teacher had just read the short episode where Chakoh, a fourteen-year-old Indian boy, discovers that Esteban, one of the group of explorers, is a slave owned by Durantes. Chakoh and Esteban had been great friends, but now Chakoh rejects him. At this point, the teacher stopped the story and began the discussion. The names of the characters had been written on the board.

Focus

The teacher planned to have the students interpret the feelings and attitudes of the people involved in the material read to them, and predict what might happen later in the story. It will be noted that this discussion strategy involves both the attitudes, feelings, and values component and the making of inferences and generalizations, including explanations.

DISCUSSION SEQUENCE

Walk the World's Rim

The following is offered as a first-rate discussion reflecting the skill of the teacher and the change in the self-image of these students as they offer their ideas with confidence.

[1] Teacher: All right, what has happened in the part of the story I have just read?

Wanda: The little boy found out that Esteban was a slave, and he was talking about a slave, and he said that he didn't have any pride or anything.

Teacher: What else has happened? Mark?

Mark: The viceroy sent for him.

[5] Teacher: The viceroy sent for whom, Mark?

Mark: For the slave.

Teacher: What was the slave's name? Do you remember, boys and girls?

All: Esteban.

Teacher: All right, what else happened in the story so far? What else has happened that you have noticed? Joe?

[10] Joe: Chakoh said that Esteban told a story. He said that he didn't say he was a slave, and the boy found out he was a slave.

Teacher: Did Esteban tell Chakoh that he was not a slave?

Joe: He didn't tell him.

Teacher: He didn't tell him anything. All right, what else has happened up to this point in the story? What about Chakoh's father? What kind of a home background had Chakoh come from?

Student: Poor and not having enough to eat.

[15] Teacher: All right. Why do you suppose this story has turned out the way it has? Yes, Joe.

Joe: Chakoh, he didn't like the slaves *'cause he lived in freedom all the time.*[13]

Teacher: Why do you think that freedom was especially important to Chakoh?

Joe: 'Cause he had it all the time.

Teacher: What other reasons? Can anyone think of any other reason why freedom might have been very important to Chakoh? Yes, Wanda.

[20] Wanda: Because his tribe, all they had was their food and their paint. They didn't have food and too much clothes and all this jazz.

Teacher: All right, then how do you suppose that Esteban felt at Chakoh's attitude? What do you suppose were the feelings that he has inside? Kathy?

Kathy: He didn't feel very good.

Teacher: How else might he have felt? Can you describe what was going on inside of Esteban? Yes, Mario?

Mario: He (Chakoh) probably felt ashamed *because he was talking bad about the slaves and everything—not knowing that Esteban was a slave.*

[25] Teacher: How else might Chakoh have felt? Raynetta?

Raynetta: He might have felt dumb *because he took the Indian boy as a slave.*

Teacher: Wanda?

Wanda: When he found out that Esteban was a slave, he was probably mad *because he had been talking about him and he accepted him as a friend.*

Teacher: How do you suppose Esteban felt when Chakoh rejected him in this way? Mario?

---

[13]In this dialogue, italics have been used to indicate that the student *has given a reason without* being asked a "why" question.

[30] Mario: He felt funny *because he thought that the Indian boy would just say, "Oh, I don't care if he's a slave or not as long as he's my friend."* He felt funny.

Teacher: All right. Any of the rest of you have ideas about how he might have felt? Darlene, how do you think Esteban felt?

Darlene: He felt sad.

Teacher: Sad. Mac?

Mac: Esteban felt sad *because the Indian boy said that he hated slaves, and didn't want him to feel sad.*

[35] Teacher: All right, Joe, what is your idea?

Joe: Esteban felt hurt 'cause *Chakoh was his only friend and Esteban, he didn't like Esteban 'cause he was a slave.*

Teacher: All right. What other feelings might Esteban have had? Wanda?

Wanda: He must have been disappointed *because if you had a friend and then you lost him real fast because you knew you was gonna lose him when he found out something you didn't want him to know about ya, you'd feel sad and disappointed.*

Teacher: Sad and disappointed. Do you have any other feelings? How might he have felt inside? Yes, Raynetta.

[40] Raynetta: He might have felt that even if he was a slave he should have accepted him anyway, in a way. He might have felt let down.

Teacher: Could you say that a little louder; I don't think that Mark could hear you.

Raynetta: He might have felt let down *because he might have thought that Esteban, (ah—I mean) the Indian boy, might maybe accepted him because he was his friend.*

Teacher: All right. Yes, Wanda.

Wanda: He must have felt that he accepted him in the first place when he didn't know he was a slave. Why couldn't he accept him now, when he found out he was?

[45] Teacher: All right. So he'd accepted him in the first place, you said, and he should have accepted him in the end. Now, I want to ask you a question about Chakoh. Remember, Chakoh lived in a very isolated Indian village. Chakoh had very little, including very little food. Now, I want you to think about what was going on inside Chakoh. Why did he react this way? Why did he have these feelings? Raynetta?

Raynetta: Maybe because the only thing he had was his freedom.

Teacher: Maybe the only thing he <u>had</u> was his freedom. Risa?

Risa: Maybe he really liked Esteban, but he was mad when he found out he was a slave.

Teacher: All right. Why might he have been mad when he found out that Esteban was a slave? What might have been some of his feelings about his finding this out?

[50] Risa: He might have been mad because Esteban didn't tell him.

Teacher: Oh, that Esteban didn't tell him. All right. Nanette, what are your feelings?

Nanette: Maybe because he didn't like to eat with slaves, and he didn't know he was a slave.

Teacher: All right. Yes, Wanda.

Wanda: When he found out that Esteban was a slave, he probably didn't want to know it because he already liked him so much and he felt unhappy 'cause he knew he couldn't stay with him if he was a slave, the way he had talked about him and everything.

[55] Teacher: All right. Raynetta?

Raynetta: He might have felt—well, he said that he didn't like slaves and then he didn't know that Esteban was a slave, and then when he found out he felt that he had let his own self down, in a way *'cause he said he didn't like them and he didn't wanta eat with them or talk to them or anything, but then now maybe* . . .

Teacher: All right. What about this man, Durantes, who was the owner of Esteban? What do you suppose Durantes felt when it was finally figured out that Esteban was a slave? Do you have any feelings about what his attitude was, Kathy?

Kathy: He probably was glad *'cause he knew that the little Indian boy was gonna turn Esteban down when he found out he was a slave.*

Teacher: All right, do you think he liked this idea of Esteban being turned away?

[60] Student: Yes.

Teacher: What kind of man was Durantes? How would you describe him? What sort of character qualities would you say he had? Risa?

Risa: Mean.

Teacher: What about you Amelio?

Amelio: Strict.

[65] Teacher: Strict. Any other ideas about this man Durantes?

Student: He was probably raised that way.

Teacher: He was raised that way? Joe?

Joe: He was cruel.

Teacher: All right. And Raynetta.

[70] Raynetta: Lazy, *because if he wasn't lazy he wouldn't have a slave for himself.*

Teacher: Oh . . . yes.

Student: He probably didn't accept other kind of people.

Teacher: All right. Now, you've gotten used to this story. You've felt a little bit how Esteban felt. Have you ever heard of anything else like this? Does this remind you of anything else you know about? Maybe a story you've heard on TV or a book you've read? Wanda?

Wanda: This is like the Negroes and the white people.

[75] Teacher: All right. Raynetta.

Raynetta: Something like the peaceful revolution.

Teacher: Something like the peaceable revolution. Do you remember the book we read about Martin Luther King and Ghandi and Thoreau? Do you think it has something to do with that? Does it remind you of a specific incident that you can think of—of something that happened to someone either in a book or in a television program—something that possibly happened to a friend of yours? Can you think of any examples? Yes, Wanda.

Wanda: Maybe you didn't like the person then. You still liked him, but you knew he didn't like you too much. And then you just tried to tell him you do and they got all mad.

Teacher: All right. How many of you have ever read the story, "Mary Jane"? Quite a few of you. Can any of you think of anything within the story, "Mary Jane", that has anything to do with what went on with Esteban? Risa?

[80] Risa: They didn't like her 'cause she was a Negro. They didn't want to sit by her or anything.

Teacher: All right. Wanda?

Wanda: They rejected her and they didn't want to do anything with her, have anything to do with her.

Teacher: Amelio, yes.

Amelio: They hated Negroes *'cause they were different colors.*

[85] Teacher: Who are you talking about?

Amelio: The Indian boy.

Teacher: The Indian boy. Because of the color. Yes?

Student: It might be as it is now—some colored people don't like Chinese. It's not all Negroes against whites—Chinese and Mexicans.

Teacher: All right, so you're talking about people rejecting people who are different. Let's think <u>again</u> about this story. How might this story have been different? What might have happened that would make what Esteban felt different? Can you think of how we could change the story? Amelio?

[90] Amelio: You mean think about how we could change the story?

Teacher: How could we change the story so the story would be different? How could this have turned out differently?

Amelio: If they were all the same.

Teacher: If they were all the same. Risa, what about you?

Risa: If the country's against slaves. (Probably means "slavery".)

[95] Teacher: That would have been different. Mac?

Mac: If all of 'em had enough food.

Teacher: If all of whom had enough food?

Mac: The Indian boy and the rest of 'em.

Teacher: All right. Wanda?

[100] Wanda: It probably would have been different if some of the Indian boy's people had been taken slaves. Then he would know what it was like to be forced to be.

Teacher: All right. Amelio?

Amelio: Show that they're all intelligent.

Teacher: They could show that they were all intelligent. Raynetta?

Raynetta: Maybe Esteban wasn't a slave.

[105] Teacher: If Esteban hadn't been a slave, that would have made the story different. Wanda?

Wanda: If he wasn't prejudiced against slaves, the Indian—or the slave—could have told him that he was a real slave.

Teacher: So, that if he hadn't been prejudiced against slaves that would have changed it. Yes, Joe.

Joe: If he wasn't prejudiced against his own people who were slaves.

Teacher: So he was prejudiced against his own people being slaves.

You remember in the story what Joe's referring to? That he wouldn't eat with those Indians who had been slaves. Why do people act in this way? Why do people have these feelings? Yes, Risa.

[110] Risa: 'Cause they were sorry for people and didn't want to have to show 'em 'cause they were proud.

Teacher: Pride. Why else might people behave in the way that Chakoh behaved toward Esteban? What would be the reasons for people behaving this way?

Wanda: Because that one thing that they had was freedom, and they probably don't have anything else of real value to them so they trade, and they feel that a person who doesn't have their freedom — they just may as well lose everything.

Teacher: All right. Mario.

Mario: They feel like some people who are shy 'cause they don't want it known that they come from a poor family and everything.

[115] Teacher: They're shy because they don't want people to know they come from a poor family. Amelio?

Amelio: They don't want like none of their friends to tease 'em for like they go play with another race of people. Well, they wouldn't wanta eat with them or play with them. They want to just play with their own race.

Teacher: Why do you suppose this is true that people only want to be with their own race? They don't want to be with people who are different. Joe?

Joe: Maybe it's prejudice.

Teacher: All right. Why do they develop these feelings? Risa?

[120] Risa: Sometimes because their parents.

Teacher: Sometimes because of their parents. Wanda?

Wanda: Sometimes because they see somebody — like somebody say something mean to a person of another color or something, and they feel that they're just talking about the whole race.

Teacher: All right.

Student: Maybe at one time or other somebody of the other race hurt you in some kind of way. I mean, made him feel bad and everything and they blame everybody for it. There's that kind.

[125] Teacher: All right. Rodell?

Rodell: It's probably what their ways are like.

Teacher: It's probably the way they're used to acting. All right boys and girls, we have been really into this story. I think you feel many things that Esteban felt and Chakoh felt. Now, I want to know how things could be different in the future? What do you suppose that we can do to change the way people feel? Is there anything that can be done to change the way people feel? Yes, Nanette.

Nanette: Let the slaves go; let them be free.

Teacher: All right. Are there slaves in the world today?

[130] Nanette: Yes.

Teacher: Could you give me an example? Are there people living in a situation like slavery? Risa what do you say to that?

Risa: Berlin.

Teacher: Berlin. Any other situations you can think of that would remind you of a situation that is like slavery? Mario?

Mario: Korea.

[135] Teacher: Korea. How can we change people's attitudes? How can we change their attitudes? Joe?

Joe: Just show 'em.

Teacher: Show them. How are we going to go about doing that? Yes, Raynetta?

Raynetta: Everybody pitch in and lend a helping hand.

Teacher: What kinds of things can we do to actually change these attitudes and behaviors? Risa?

[140] Risa: They can show different kinds of things people can do.

Teacher: All right. Can anyone think of a specific example? All right. Raynetta?

Raynetta: Be proud of what you are and not of what you're not.

Teacher: Be proud of what you are. Mario?

Mario: Tell 'em that they're not the only ones that has feelings.

[145] Teacher: All right. Amelio?

Amelio: Show 'em that everyone is the same. They're all human beings.

Teacher: Any other ideas about what we can do to change people's attitudes and the way we feel about things? This is a problem, isn't it? It's something we really want to consider. We want to understand not only how Esteban felt but how Chakoh felt, and why people have certain ideas they have. If you examine, first of all, and think about why they have their ideas and why people behave the way they do, maybe then we'll be able to know what to do to change this. Now I hope you enjoyed this story, and this is all we are going to do today. I know that some of you are interested in reading what is going to happen in this relationship in the end, and that will be interesting to find out. Yes, Nanette.

Nanette: The Indian boy won't be talking to the slave.

Teacher: The Indian won't be talking to the slave? What do some of the rest of you think about what's going to happen in this book? This is not the end of the book. Mark?

[150] Mark: They might make friends.

Teacher: They might make friends. Can anyone else have ideas? Yes, Rosemary?

Rosemary: Turn out good.

Teacher: You think it's going to turn out good? How about you, Wanda?

Wanda: He might start thinking on slaves in another way.

[155] Teacher: He might start thinking about slaves in another way. Joe?

Joe: He might feel ashamed about the way he was acting, and he might make friends.

Teacher: All right. Yes?

Student: He might find that freedom's not the only thing he can have, but the way he was brought up — that was the only thing that was really important to him; I mean to keep pushing on.

Teacher: I see. Risa.

[160] Risa: Esteban might explain why he was dishonest to Chakoh.

Teacher: All right. Lynette?

Lynette: They might be friends again, and that man might get mad at him and the boy.

Teacher: Oh, Durantes. Durantes might be angry if they made friends. Mario.

Mario: In the near future he might have a dream that something happened to the slave and then he might wake up, and then he might find him, and then they might make friends.

[165] Teacher: Oh, OK. Yes, Amelio.

Amelio: Maybe the man who owns the slave will let him go, and then the Indian boy and the slave will make up and after they'll just start traveling to where they were going.

Teacher: All right. Wanda, what do you think?

Wanda: When they get to Mexico City he might see how other slaves are treated and how mean their masters are really to them, so he could see the real truth about it and then they'd probably make up.

Teacher: Reggie, what about you?

[170] Reggie: I think that Esteban might, I mean the person who sent for him for chores, might keep him there and make him a slave.

Teacher: You know, I don't think that I could really hear that clearly. Could you say it again?

Reggie: The man from the church who sent for him might keep him there to be a slave.

Teacher: What else? Nanette, do you have an idea?

Nanette: The boy that's a slave — the man might, if they make up — the man might give him some medicine so he could die.

[175] Teacher: Oh. Well, you've had many interesting ideas about what's going to happen in this story. And I hope that you've enjoyed to-day exploring what was going on inside of Esteban and inside Chakoh. Thank you very much. You've been very good in your answers. You've had a lot of good things to say. We'll continue reading the story to-morrow.

POINTS FOR THOUGHT

*Walk the World's Rim***

1. As you read the discussion sequence, "Walk the World's Rim", fill in the numbers at the point where the discussion moves from:

Analysis of episode to feelings	_____ (to)	_____
Why these people felt as they did	_____ (to)	_____
Identification with others	_____ (to)	_____
How things could have been different	_____ (to)	_____
How we change how people feel	_____ (to)	_____
Predicting the outcome	_____ (to)	_____

2. Identify sequences which provide evidence that this class not only can think but seems to show an interest in responding to the

**See Chapter 9, page 107.

thought-provoking questions of the teacher. Sequences and what they indicate:

_____

_____

_____

_____

As Others See It

INTRODUCTION

THE questions in this chapter refer to the questions and exercises enumerated in the "Points for Thought" sections, which are cited by name in the various headings that follow. Readers are urged to go back to the "Points for Thought" and reconsider them in light of others' views.

CHAPTER 1: SIGNALS OF DISCOMFORT IN CHILDREN

As you responded to the questions about classroom atmosphere, did any of these occur to you:

(*1*) Shock, disbelief, surprise, rejection, disapproval?
   – Did you wish you could have heard the tape to note the tone of the teacher's voice?
   – Did you wonder whether this might have been a very young teacher whose life experience would not have prepared her to anticipate the responses several children gave?
   – Did it occur to you that some of these children's parents may have had only one hot substance to give a child before he took a long walk through the ranch to the bus stop and then a long ride to school?

(*2*) Could it be that few of us are used to asking open-ended questions? Are we as teachers too often certain we know what is "right" or possible for a parent to do for a child?

(*3*) Frightened, hostile, ashamed (as though Mary's mother were doing something wrong), disobedient?
   – Did it occur to you that Willie became creative and demonstrated high-level thinking?

93

(4) Most teachers felt Ms. Milton realized what was happening when she talked with Billy. In discussing the tape, Ms. Milton said, "You're talking about the children being trapped. I'm the one who was trapped. I'm used to telling them what they should be eating and drinking for good health."

(5) The teacher might discover that his/her question was vague or misunderstood:

− The teacher might note a stammer, hesitation, or tension in a child's voice.

− The tape might make the teacher aware that he/she is showing no interest in what some children have said, while showing much interest in the contributions of others.

− Several teachers reported that while listening to a tape, they became critical of a pace that they once considered "lively". One teacher said she used to close a discussion with "Thanks, that was a good, lively discussion." Now I'm critical of that liveliness. They were all just popping off, never giving reason or proof for anything. Also, I never checked to see how many different children entered the discussion. I realize now that such answering left many children out entirely. On the other hand, a number of teachers were happily surprised to see how well they had been doing all along.

(6) Facial expression, no comment, ignoring a child, or failing to give support when others criticize a child's work may well be interpreted by the child as disapproval or rejection of his/her contribution. On the other hand, facial expression or a pat on the head may mean acceptance.

All classrooms that support productive thinking will not be organized and managed in the same way. Teachers are individuals and each must find that atmosphere in which he/she can successfully assume that all-important role of discussion leader.

CHAPTER 2: LISTING, GROUPING, AND LABELING

Here are points to consider in deciding whether to have young children draw a picture that illustrates the focus of the discussion to be held:

• For the young child, drawing to focus serves as making notes does for an older student.

- Pre-planning promotes independent thinking.
- His/her own picture is a source of security as to "what to say" when called upon.
- The variety of drawings helps to prevent "chains" (copying what others say).
- The variety provides a wider assortment of items for the children to group.

As you responded to the questions on developing concepts, did questions such as these arise in your mind:

Question (1): Where would Dr. Taba consider a vague "Let's talk about your picture" as being appropriate?

 — Dr. Taba would probably advise a teacher to use such an open invitation to a child when she knows the child has had little experience with books, or his/her development is still at the level of only identifying objects in a picture, or the child has difficulty expressing his/her ideas in a group.
 — Also, there are many times when the teacher's objective is focused on the picture itself — the colors the child chose, and why; what feelings the child had about colors. Does it make him/her think of fun? A poem? A story? etc.

Question (3): Did it occur to you that the teacher's purpose in giving the children a reason for grouping is to teach them a way of organizing? Grouping is not an end in itself.

 — You would not have been able to classify the responses you charted unless the child had given the reason for his grouping. Too often we attribute adult reasons as the basis of a child's response.
 — A teacher told of asking seven year olds to arrange a handful of rocks into smaller groups. He was impressed with one child who said, "I've grouped mine according to age." "That's interesting," said the teacher. "Tell me more." "Oh," said the seven year old, "you know — big rocks and little rocks."
 — Each time the child is asked to give a title for a story or to write a summary statement or to organize a notebook, he/she is being asked to group information and to condense lists or a series of events into more economical or abstract terms. It is the process that the child is learning that is important.
 — As you read through sequences [49]–[53], [77], [78], and

[80], were you impressed with the way the teacher handled two obviously very different children? Did you recognize that she was supporting Laurie who needed reassurance and David S. who was frustrated?

Note: When would the children have use for abstract words or concepts? Dr. Taba would stress the importance of students learning the new aspects or dimensions of a concept as it grows, as shown in the examples given in Points for Thought.

At times when older students are noting the change in the meaning of a word, it is relevant to look at the history of the word. I recall a bright seventh-grade class, not easily motivated, who became intrigued when a teacher showed them that "bonfire" derived from the burning of bones. They began to read a dictionary more carefully. It gave them a glimpse of a new world of study.

CHAPTER 3: A TEACHER'S FIRST EFFORT TO ELICIT GENERALIZATIONS

As you responded to the question about leading children to infer and generalize, did any of these occur to you:

Questions (1)–(4): The teacher did a splendid job in the sequence of questions that led the children to generalize well on their first effort. However, the question that sets the focus at the beginning of the discussion always needs a careful look. Is it vague? Which category of "people" am I really after? Might the word "need" influence the child's response? See "Chris" in entry [64].

Question (5): The teacher does not lead by saying, "What can you tell me about the way the nomad travels?" She merely asks them to look at the information and make a statement. This requires more of the child and gives him/her a wider choice.

- Did you note that two children gave or inferred comparisons in their statements?
- Did you note that one child qualified the "people" he was referring to?

Questions (7)–(9): As you identified problems, did you consider that the manner in which the resource material is written may be doing all the thinking for the children? If books, films, and other materials do the generalizing for the children, then what the child repeats is only memory work. Teachers who are interested in the students learning the process of thinking should inform publishers and filmmakers of their criteria for proper materials as they preview for purchase. Parents should be kept informed when a different approach to study is instituted or enhanced. Maybe parents can prevent teachers from receiving reports copied from the encyclopedia at home.

The teacher conducting this third-grade discussion emphasized mutual listening among the children. Using the names of children often when giving credit not only enhances the child's self-concept but lends importance to what all children say. There's an old saying: "The sweetest music to anyone's ears is the sound of their own name."

—Did you consider how you might handle a situation in which a child takes a premature leap into generalizing, as Lisa does in the following sequence? (A third-grade class had studied a culture where all members of the family participated in earning the living. The teacher planned to have the class compare those families with the children's own families.)

Teacher: What kinds of things do your families do together?
Child: Live in the same house.
Child: We have dinner together.
Child: We go places together.
Lisa: Everybody has their own way of thinking and their own way of doing things.
Teacher: Well, could we——
Lisa: Well, some of the people, it's effect—it's their way of doing things affected by education, religion, and work, but uh, I think that everybody has his own ideas and ways of doing things without that.
Teacher: Very good. We'll keep that idea and bring it back again, because this is part of what we're working toward today.

The teacher said it was hard to evaluate the contributions of Lisa because she never knew when she was quoting her parents, who were sociologists. However, the teacher said the other children never seemed to be influenced by anything Lisa said.

CHAPTER 3: FORMULATING QUESTIONS

(*1*) In preparing the question related to the data that had been charted, did it occur to you:
- to check your focusing question for clarity?
- to consider what you might ask if a student overgeneralizes, such as, "People are happy to get new ideas from other nations"?

(*2*) Did you formulate questions to get at the reasons for a child's inference or generalization?

(*3*) If it's appropriate, did you plan to ask the students to recall situations previously studied where ideas and achievement flowed from one culture to another, e.g., between Spain and Aztec and Inca Empires, often studied in the sixth grade?

(*4*) Did you wonder how children react to being asked questions that seek to lift the level of their thinking?
- Children seem to become aware of a teacher's style of teaching. A member of the testing team reported that as he distributed a test to a seventh grader at a middle school, the student remarked, "This is the way Mr. W. (his sixth-grade teacher) used to teach." "How is that?" asked the tester. The student replied, "He was always interested in what we thought about things."
- The research team constructed a pupil reaction questionnaire of twenty-five items which was administered to both curriculum classroom and control classroom in the project research. "Curriculum" pupils indicated significantly greater liking for the following curriculum-related items:

> Being asked by teacher and classmates to explain why I think or feel as I do.
> Working on things that have no simple, clear answer.
> Having to figure out why things happen.
> Having the teacher ask me questions.
> Organizing a lot of information in a way that makes sense.

One teacher showed her class a film on ancient Greece, then asked, "What happened?" She wrote a myriad of responses at random on the chalkboard. She then asked her students to write three generalizations they could make about early Greece. They became convinced that organizing data was worthwhile.

CHAPTER 3: WHAT WOULD HAPPEN IF . . . ?

As you responded to the questions about leading students to consider whether generalizations already arrived at are applicable in a given situation, did any of the following occur to you:

Questions (2) and (3): Question (7) is an example of a "leading question". It puts words in the mouth of the student and might well have caused the discussion to lose focus by considering how the situation might have been prevented, rather than solving the problems.

- In suggesting another question did you consider inviting other children to add to what Carol, in entry [4], had said? It is early in the discussion and helps to extend participation if others get in early.

Question (4): Did you consider that the differences between Haiti and Argentina are too great to be handled without depth study? The teacher said that the child who mentioned Haiti's efforts to regain tourist trade had read widely on the history of Haiti.

Question (5): Did you consider this a point at which you would have asked Tonia the source of her information that "almost everybody in the United States is a middle-class worker"? Would you plan to have Tonia or a group research this point and report to the class?

CHAPTER 3: WHY WOULDN'T IT HAPPEN?

(*1*) In planning your sequence of questions, did you consider:
- eliciting the similarities in the two situations?
- eliciting the differences in the two situations inviting divergent points of view?

(2) In formulating the question, did you consider these conditions:
- time and why it could be important?
- where the two products are found and the difference that makes?
- the source of the equipment and where the workers who make it live?
- how the two products are/were transported and what difference that would make?
- who took the gold from the earth in the days of the '49ers and where did they live?

- who takes the oil from the earth today?
- when the miner who took the gold from the earth was paid for his work, where he spent it?
- where the money for shovels, small rails, and mine cars came from and where the money stayed?
- when the equipment for oil wells is paid for where the money goes?

(3) Did you consider having someone from the area (farmer on the property where oil was discovered; worker who checked equipment) act as a resource person on these important conditions?

It is not unusual for children (and adults) to totally ignore facts if those facts negate an explanation or a prediction they have in mind. Such facts are counter-intuitive. Individuals will do it in science as well as in social studies. Compliment the child who raises questions about something that appears in a book or is said that seems to contradict what they know or think they know.

CHAPTER 4: EVALUATING STUDENTS' GENERALIZATIONS

The majority of teachers who evaluated the sampling of generalizations made by sixth graders rated them as follows:

+(highest rating): numbers 2, 4, 6, and 7
−(lowest rating): numbers 1, 3, 8, and 10

As you examined the generalizations, note that the four rated highest (above) not only contained the largest number of abstract terms (four or five), but also examples of tentativeness, cause and effect, and precision.

Look again at the following statements:

[5] Although the teachers did not rate it high, it does contain an example of precision and spontaneous comparison.

[11] The student who wrote this statement used three abstract words and an example of precision.

[12] Here we find two abstract words, and a dependent clause that gives precision to the statement.

When you are examining titles students have given to stories, notebooks, etc., consider (1) inclusiveness, (2) abstractness, and (3) not the least, originality.

Examples of summary sentences by sixth graders after they had read a short episode of a family's visit to the "home town":

It was about people going home and finding the old customs make you happier than city customs.

All our modern things may not bring happiness.

CHAPTER 5: IMPROVING STATEMENTS MADE BY STUDENTS

As you responded to the questions in Points for Thought, did any of the following occur to you?

Question (1): The children might well think of a label (such as "condition") as belonging only to the situation in which he/she learned it, for example, "road conditions".

– Seizing opportunities to use any label in a variety of situations introduces the student to the flexibility of our language.
– Dr. Taba reminded us continually that children discover ideas, not words. She felt it was a dreary waste of time trying to get children to remember a particular word. If you feel they have an understanding of the concept, give them the word.
– Without using Dr. Taba's terminology, these fourth graders listed criteria they thought would improve the generalizations they had made:
  • *precision:* Is the word "need" right for this statement?
  • *abstractness:* "Put all of them (four items) together."
  • *tentativeness:* "We don't know it all, just part of it."
  • *comparing:* "modern workers" as opposed to "workers in earlier times"
  • and important, though not listed in the criteria, *"We helped each other."*

The sequence in which the children discussed the word "need" also contains an example of divergent thinking. The discussion was centered on the following generalization written on the chalkboard: <u>People of the world need the products California grows and processes</u>.

Teacher: Yesterday Lorrie gave us this very good statement.
Ben: I'd say "Almost everyone in the world . . ."
Teacher: Why do you think that would improve it?

Ben: Because, like with oranges. Maybe like Florida, they don't need our oranges.

Cynthia: Some, we could say some.

Lorrie: Well, people in the world need our products that they don't grow themselves.

Teacher: What is Lorrie telling us when she says, "People who don't grow their products themselves"?

Ben: She's not saying just some, but if they don't have it.

Teacher: Yes, she's telling which people need them. Let's look at the word "need". What do you think of the word "need"?

There followed a sequence in which several words were offered as substitutes for the word "need". They seemed to be accepted by all except Lorrie.

Lorrie: Sometimes they do need it . . . maybe not need . . . but it might make them healthier and happier, and so I would still say that people who don't grow California products need them because it makes them healthier and happier.

In a conference, the teacher talked about Lorrie. "Lorrie is a child who listens and thinks about suggestions. If she understands the point being made and agrees, she accepts it completely; if she doesn't, she rejects it. It's a joy to observe her independence in a nine-year-old." Lorrie used a great deal of body language as she talked. One day the teacher asked her to explain how she thought of a "label". "Well," said Lorrie, "it's like the label is a big word that has a lot of little words inside it." She stood up, made an umbrella of her left hand and said, "Say this is Materials" (then putting her right-hand fingers under the umbrella, she continued), "and if you're thinking about Indians, my fingers could be clay or tules, but if you're thinking about '49ers they could be water or logs."

Discussions letting children in on criteria take time, but can be understood at the elementary level. What is more important than having children know, understand, and use those criteria by which their speech and writing will be judged by the time they reach high school?

Question (3): As you reread the students' responses in entries [33], [37], and [46], did you find examples of good thinking that agreed with the opinions of other teachers who offered those shown below? (From the discussion sequence "What Would Happen If . . . ?", pages 34–35):

[33] Jeff: *applying other information, comparing, generalizing about the expectation of the populace*

[37] Cody: *that people are being exploited,* or *that it is happening not just in some foreign country, but in ours also*

[46] Wendy: *arrives at a generalization: qualifies her statement*

CHAPTER 6: SUCCESS WHEN THE POOR READER IS INVITED TO THINK

After rereading the first four exchanges in the discussion, did any of the following occur to you?

Question (1): The focusing question has two sides. (Do you think these people would discover these things, etc.?) The teacher allows Margie to keep explaining one side of the argument.

Questions (2) and (3): Ryan is responding to the first question even though the teacher has not repeated it. Many children would have lost sight of the fact that there might be two sides to the question.

The second question might well have been "What makes you think so?"; then followed with "Does anyone have a different idea about this?" and "What makes you think so?"

Questions (4) and (5): Even though the children spoke to only one side of the question for some time, there were examples of good thinking in what they said:

[4] Margie expresses tentativeness a couple of times.

[5] June gave an unelicited reason; spoke tentatively.

[11] Mike gave a reason autonomously.

[12] Ryan gave his reason for thinking in the form of a question; however, it was not as though he was asking for information but as a dare for anyone to challenge his idea.

Question (6): Ryan seemed to know he had said something so good he surprised the teacher. He was certainly pleased with himself.

CHAPTER 6: DEBORAH MODIFIES HER THINKING

Questions (1)–(3): Did you notice that:

- Deborah was the first to speak and that her response was in no way qualified?
- by response [15] she was saying it would take time
- by [18] she was noting the differences between how young and old feel about change?
- Ronald's reference to their study of Hong Kong may have triggered in her mind a generalization about people holding on to some of the ways of their ancestors for a time?
- the children were the ones commenting about feelings; the teacher gave no new information or opinion, but asked the questions that led them to make inferences about the feelings of others? This is the point at which Deborah re-entered the discussion [11].

Questions (4) and (5): No doubt you located the four reasons that were given autonomously. One more reason was given in response to the teacher's "why?" Usually we don't ask "why?" when a reason has just been given; however, it seems to me to be a very thoughtful insight.

In addition to the reasons being given autonomously, the responses provided examples of good thinking:

[3] Ronald: *recalled a similar situation, spoke tentatively*

[8] Freddy: *gave his reason tentatively*

[9] Brenda: *spoke tentatively*

[17] Mark: *spoke tentatively*

[18] Deborah: *made a splendid comparison between old and young, and [11] extended Brenda's remarks by adding an explanation*

Remember that these responses were from children who were considered poor readers, but that the intake of information had been rich for eight-year-olds. There were a couple of important aspects in this short sequence which should be noted: (a) Deborah's prediction [2] immediately met with rejection [3], but (b) she re-entered the discussion [11], and (c) she modified her thinking by adding a very important factor of change—time [15]. It may be necessary for the teacher to invite a student whose contribution has been rejected to re-enter the discussion with such questions as: (so and so), could you add to what Bill has just said? Could you give us an example?

CHAPTER 7: MATCHING ROLES AND QUESTIONS/RESPONSES

When teachers examined the different roles Ms. Kelley assumed (to set focus, reset and change focus; to support and to elicit clarification), their remarks centered on her skill as a supporter, such as:

- There was a point where Ms. Kelley might have used firm, stern language and acted as a disciplinarian; instead she used her skill to involve the children in broadening the fault of unreliability and seeing how all of them were improving.
- Her self-discipline in not being "preachy", such as, "Listen to your parents" and, in a positive manner, addressed the problems of the group as something both parents and children work on as children grow up.

Did you notice that these fourth graders in a low socioeconomic neighborhood of a large city are quite adept at summarizing and expressing a point of view?

CHAPTER 8: PURSUING A PROBLEM, SENSITIVITY TO THE FEELINGS OF OTHERS, AND OFFERING SOLUTIONS

Questions (1)–(5): As you read the section [1]–[60] of the discussion sequence, "Eva, the New Girl from Puerto Rico," did it occur to you that this situation was one the teacher felt she had to deal with immediately? There was no time to plan, to consider what dimensions of the problem might arise and how they should be handled. Now that you have had time to examine the discussion, did you, as others have, consider any of the following:

- having the child who has experienced "name-calling" perhaps identify with Eva by asking, "Has anything like this ever happened to you?" and "How did you feel?"
- asking the students such a question as, "Why do you suppose people act the way these children are acting when they are name calling?"

Question (6): As you read the suggestions the children made for correcting the problem, did you note the originality and the maturity of their responses?

Episode from Film

- As you developed a question sequence, did you consider the order of the questions as carefully as the content they were planned to elicit?
- Did you include questions to deal with the feelings of all persons involved in the episode?
- Did you use a question that would get at an expression of feelings from students who had anything similar happen to them?
- Did you use questions that get at the reasons children have for the responses they are giving?

Human relations usually deal with quite sensitive areas. For that reason, Dr. Taba suggested the use of books, films, etc., because they are less personal. You might consider letting the students write their reactions to episodes. Teachers have used different approaches:

- Some teachers did not at any time suggest to the students that they might share their writings.
- Some provided time for those who wished to share with the class.
- Some students could share in small groups if they wished.

All agreed that when a child writes his/her personal reactions, he/she must know the teacher will hold it in confidence.

Observer's note: All this takes planning. Sometime a child will alert you to a factor you have forgotten as seen in the following dialogue:

Teacher: (ready to read an episode to fourth graders) Listen carefully to what happened in this episode. After I finish reading, we will list on the board just what happened. We will not discuss the story because I don't want you to be influenced by what someone else says. Each of you will write how you think so-and-so felt and how you would have felt.

Ben: Mr. C., we can tell how you feel about what happened by the way you read it.

CHAPTER 8: WALK THE WORLD'S RIM

Many teachers remarked about the mature thinking they found in this discussion carried on by teacher and students who would not, or could not, cooperate in September. Did you note the following:

- On thirteen occasions, the students gave reasons for their different responses without being asked a "Why?" question.
- Several children try to identify the feelings of the slave.
- A child initiates a new focus which the teacher picks up.
- The students constantly use such tentative terms as *may have, probably, maybe.*
- The teacher has to refocus only twice (adults in a discussion rarely do that well).
- Children initiate reasons for other people's attitudes or actions several times.
- Several students extended a former speaker's point without the teacher asking, "Would someone like to add to so-and-so's point?"
- One child asked for clarification.
- When the teacher asked, "What do some of the rest of you think is going to happen in this book?", the children came up with twelve predictions.

Most of the teachers have said they enjoyed the sequences dealing with feelings and the reasons for the feeling ([21] to [73]) and the sequence where the students predict what will happen ([149]–[174]).

In both sequences, the students were thinking independently, expressing divergent views, and most of them were speaking fluently and in full sentences. Not once in this discussion did the teacher have to ask a child to be quiet.

Baron, J. B. and E. Stenberg. 1986. *Teaching Thinking Skills; Theory and Practice.* W. H. Freeman.

Belth, Marc. 1977 (out of print). *The Process of Thinking.* David McKay.

Beyer, Barry. 1988. *Developing a Thinking Skills Program.* Allyn (Longwood Div.).

Beyer, Barry. 1987. *Practical Strategies for the Teaching of Thinking.* Allyn (Longwood Div.).

Beyer, Barry. 1991. *Teaching Thinking Skills; A Handbook for Elementary School Teachers.* Allyn.

Bruner, J. R. 1986. *Actual Minds, Possible Worlds.* Harvard U.

Brunner, J. R. 1973. *Beyond Information Given; Studies in the Psychology of Knowing.* Norton.

Chuska, K. R. 1986. "Teaching the Process of Thinking," *Phi Delta Kappan.*

Fraenkel, J. R. 1969. "A Curriculum Model for the Social Studies," *Social Education,* 33:41–47.

Fraenkel, J. R. 1969. *Helping Students Think and Value: Strategies for Teaching Social Studies. 2nd Ed.* Prentice Hall.

Fraenkel, J. R., A. McNaughton, N. E. Wallen and M. Durkin. 1969. "Improving Elementary-School Social Studies: An Idea-Oriented Approach," *The Elementary School Journal,* 70:154–163.

Goswami, D. and P. Stillman. 1987. *Reclaiming the Classroom: Teacher Research as an Agency of Change.* Boynton/Cook Publ.

McPeck, J. et al. 1990. *Teaching Critical Thinking.* Routledge.

Norris, S. 1966 (out of print). *Classroom Question.* Harper & Row.

Norris, S. 1992. *The Generalizability of Critical Thinking.* Teachers College Press.

Norris, S. and R. H. Ennis. 1989. *Evaluating Critical Thinking.* Midwest Publications.

Paul, Richard. 1990. *Critical Thinking Handbook (Gr. K–3): A Guide for Remodeling Lesson Plans in Language Arts, Social Studies and Science.* Center for Critical Thinking.

Paul, Richard. 1987. *Critical Thinking Handbook (Gr. 4–6): A Guide for Remodeling Lesson Plans in Language Arts, Social Studies and Science.* Center for Critical Thinking.

Paul, Richard. 1989. *Critical Thinking Handbook (Gr. 6–9): A Guide for Remodeling Lesson Plans in Language Arts, Social Studies and Science.* Center for Critical Thinking.

Schiever, S. 1991. *A Comprehensive Approach to Teaching Thinking.* Allyn.

Scriven, M. 1977. *Reasoning*. McGraw-Hill.

Taba, H. 1967. "Implementing Thinking as an Objective in Social Studies," in *Effective Thinking in the Social Studies, 37th Yearbook,* Jean Fair and Fannie Shaftel, eds., Washington, D.C. National Council for the Social Studies, pp. 25–49.

Taba, H., M. Durkin, J. R. Fraenkel and A. McNaughton. 1971. *A Teacher's Handbook to Elementary Social Studies: An Inductive Approach. 2nd ed.* Addison Wesley.

Taba, H. and F. Elzey. 1964. "Teaching Strategies and Thought Processes," *Teachers College Record,* 65:524–534.

Wallen, N. E., M. Durkin, J. R. Fraenkel, A. McNaughton and E. I. Sawin. 1969. "Development of a Comprehensive Model for Social Studies for Grades One through Eight, Inclusive of Procedures for Implementation and Dissemination," Final Report, Project No. 5-1314, Washington, D.C.: U.S. Office of Education.

Whimbey, A. 1975 (out of print). *Intelligence Can Be Taught.* E. P. Dutton.

Wilson, J. 1970. *Thinking with Concepts.* Cambridge U. Press.